Cities in Time

Cities in Time

Temporary Urbanism and the Future of the City

ALI MADANIPOUR

Bloomsbury Academic
An imprint of Bloomsbury Publishing Plc

B L O O M S B U R Y
LONDON · OXFORD · NEW YORK · NEW DELHI · SYDNEY

Bloomsbury Academic

An imprint of Bloomsbury Publishing Plc

50 Bedford Square
London
WC1B 3DP
UK

1385 Broadway
New York
NY 10018
USA

www.bloomsbury.com

BLOOMSBURY and the Diana logo are trademarks of Bloomsbury Publishing Plc

First published 2017

British Library Cataloguing-in-Publication Data
A catalogue record for this book is available from the British Library.

ISBN:	HB:	978-1-4742-2072-9
	PB:	978-1-4742-2071-2
	ePDF:	978-1-4742-2074-3
	ePub:	978-1-4742-2073-6

Library of Congress Cataloging-in-Publication Data
Names: Madanipour, Ali, author.
Title: Cities in time : temporary urbanism and the future of the city / Ali Madanipour.
Description: New York : Bloomsbury Academic, 2017. |
Includes bibliographical references.
Identifiers: LCCN 2016029692 | ISBN 9781474220712 (paperback) |
ISBN 9781474220729 (hardback)
Subjects: LCSH: Urbanization. | Time–Social aspects. | BISAC: ARCHITECTURE /
General. | ARCHITECTURE / Criticism. | ARCHITECTURE / Urban & Land Use Planning.
Classification: LCC HT361 .M33 2017 | DDC 307.76–dc23
LC record available at https://lccn.loc.gov/2016029692

Typeset by Integra Software Services Pvt. Ltd.
Printed and bound in India

Contents

List of Figures

All images are by the author, apart from Figure 6.11, which is kindly supplied by Artgineering, Rotterdam.

1

The Multiple Times of the City

From pop-up shops to street festivals, from mobile buildings to temporary gardens, the temporary construction and use of urban space is widely discussed and practised, as part of a growing international trend that can be found in different fields, where many invest their hopes and energies in what they think of as innovative and fashionable. The aim of this book is to develop a critical analysis of temporary urbanism, trying to understand, analyse and problematize it. The main questions that need answering are about what it is, the role it plays and the effect it may have on the future of the urban environment: whether it is an interim fashion aimed at filling short-term economic gaps or a reflection of structural change and an instrument of transformation with long-term impacts. If it is associated with the multiplication and acceleration of temporality in the city, does it make life more precarious or more creative?

The title of the American pavilion at the 2012 Venice Architecture Biennale was *Spontaneous Interventions*, which received a Special Mention for national participation from the Biennale's Golden Lion jury. The exhibition was subtitled *Design Actions for the Common Good* and included 124 projects initiated by designers, artists and activists devoted to the improvement of urban areas, described by its initiators as 'a new, democratic design movement that is growing across the country' (Institute for Urban Design, 2013). The projects ranged across a variety of scales and themes, from guerrilla gardening to a pop-up chapel and from converting a street into a green space to placing historical markers around the town, and even including the occupy movement's turning streets into protest spaces. The exhibition was selected through open competition by the Bureau of Educational and Cultural Affairs of the US Department of State, aiming to showcase 'the excellence, vitality, diversity, and innovation' of the American architecture on a global stage (Institute for Urban Design, 2013). As the American organizers explained in the introductory essay for their entry at the Venice Biennale, 'Provisional, informal, guerrilla, insurgent, DIY, hands-on, informal, unsolicited, unplanned, participatory, tactical, micro, open-source – these are just a few of the words floating around to describe a type of interventionist urbanism sweeping through cities around the world' (Lang Ho, 2013).

What the contents of the American exhibition at Venice Biennale, a festival in London's Regent Street, Parisian beaches, a container building in the centre of Vienna and the British pop-up shops share is that they are all temporary events in urban space. The flavour of events on London's Regent Street is decidedly commercial, where the Regent Street Partnership sets up frequent events throughout the year as an encouragement for people to visit the fashionable shopping street, which already attracts 7.5 million tourists a year. The events range from a two-week 'food safari' to a Fashion Night Out, temporary traffic-free days and working with the Royal Institute of British Architects to offer young architects the opportunity to design prestigious shop windows (Regent Street Partnership, 2013). Meanwhile, the municipality of Paris has turned some parts of the banks of the Seine into sandy beaches each summer since 2002. Car traffic is stopped, deck chairs and ice cream sellers appear, concerts and games are set up, water sport and open air attractions operate, all for four weeks in July and August (Paris Municipality, 2013). Meanwhile, pop-up retailing is a global trend that is embraced by small entrepreneurs and large corporations alike. In the recent years, Bob Dylan, Chanel and Coca-Cola have all opened a pop-up shop in central London, while the luxury hotels Dorchester and Claridge's ran pop-up restaurants (London Pop-ups, 2012).

These interventions, the spread and occurrence of which have been widening and accelerating with time, are widely different in location, scale and purpose, performed by the public, private and civil society actors. On the surface, they could not be more different from one another. What all these interventions share, however, is their ephemerality; they are all events that exemplify the temporary construction and use of urban space. While many of these activities are not new, it is noticeable that they have mushroomed in recent years in different types of activity and different countries, becoming a fashionable international trend. If it is such an emerging strong trend, an important question is: why? What do those who are involved in a short-lived activity expect from it? What is it, a sign of a fleeting fashion in a consumerist society, a recurring sign of endemic crises of the market economy or an existential condition of modernity magnified by the global economy?

As reflected in the American entry at the Venice Biennale, the theme of temporary urbanism is becoming increasingly important in architectural and urban design discourse, but it tends to be examined in an empirical and practical way. Some studies have focused on ephemerality and transience in specific cities: either tracing their rapid transformation, as in Houston (Scardino et al., 2004), or on the proposals for their transformation, as in

Luxembourg (Koolhaas et al., 2008), or on an architect's projects (Tschumi, 2010). More often, however, the temporary use of urban space is advocated as an opportunity for change and as a critique of fixed rules, rigid master planning and long-term strategies.

A number of such texts have come out of German-speaking countries for a decade, in particular Berlin, which had faced structural change after the unification and has been the site of vibrant cultural experiments. While some focus on conveying the sense of transience in a place, such as the photographs of Berlin clubs (Eberle et al., 2001) or the experience of tourism and migration in the city (Bauman et al., 2010; Weitzel, 2011), most are interested in the temporary use of space: the pioneering role of Berlin in finding alternative uses for its underused spaces (Jovis, 2007), the experimental projects for its public spaces (Zander, 2008), but also of examples from elsewhere to show the application of trial and error methods in opposition to long-range planning (Temel and Haydn, 2006; Bishop and Williams, 2012), the reuse of vacant sites and waste lands (Oswalt et al., 2013) and the recycling of underused spaces (Ziehl et al., 2012). In addition to the temporary uses of space, temporary buildings are also discussed, such as the imperial expositions held in fin-de-siècle London, Paris and Berlin (Geppert, 2013), or examples of current temporary buildings such as pavilions, fair stands, container-architecture, stage sets, installations and temporary housing solutions (Jodidio, 2011).

Analysing temporary urbanism may start by listing the diverse instances of short-lived events, arriving at the conclusion that it is a significant new trend in urban societies, and describing the details of its different forms and the place and frequency of their occurrence. Such an analysis would offer the examples of these short-lived events and in a way produce a catalogue of such events. This would be a valuable exercise in providing concrete examples of what might be considered to be the constituting elements of an innovative trend. My attempt, however, has been focused on developing a theoretical interpretation of this trend. The main aim of this book is to understand and explain the phenomenon of temporary urbanism through a critical and theoretical evaluation of this trend and its implications for the future of cities.

Urban processes and temporal change

The increased frequency of short-term events, in particular the temporary construction and use of space, has become known as temporary urbanism. This book develops a theoretical and critical analysis of this global trend by locating it in the philosophical concepts of time, the economic and technological processes of global change, and the social and personal experiences of life in the city. It offers a critical evaluation of temporary urbanism, the context in which it has come about, how it causes anxiety and precarity, but also how it may include creative potentials for the future of the city. It argues that temporary urbanism should be understood through the dynamics of urban temporality: how time unfolds in the city, locating temporary urbanism in the wider context of the multiple and multi-layered timeframes and lifecycles of the city, and opening up broader perspectives on how time is embedded and expressed in the life of the city. The substantive, relational and intuitive concepts of time are all at work to construct an order of events from a series of spatiotemporal fragments.

The approach that I have adopted is to combine a political economy and a cultural analysis of urban processes (Madanipour, 1996; 2003; 2007; 2014), which helps undertake a critical and multidimensional understanding of the subject of temporary urbanism (Lefebvre, 1991; Foucault, 2002, 2008). I have drawn on relational and intuitive concepts of time to develop a critique of substantive time and instrumental temporality, which frame the conditions of possibility of temporary urbanism. I have used a dialectical methodology, which would provide a critical analysis of how these different forms of temporality intersect, but also opens up new pathways to look for creative potential of events (Badiou, 2005, 2009). While focusing on temporality, I have analysed it in a close relation to spatiality, as time and space cannot be treated separately, and as the term suggests, temporary urbanism refers to both time and space at the same time.

As temporary urbanism is primarily a temporal designation for urban processes, it is evident that a starting point for such a theoretical articulation would be the concept of time. Ephemerality of temporary interventions in urban space leads to an exploration of time and temporality: how it is affected by the processes of, and responses to, acceleration associated with globalization, and how it includes both precarity and creativity. The book examines the notions of time, the economic and technological changes that have accelerated the pace of urban life, and the impact of change on the natural world and social life. While these changes bring about precarity for the vulnerable, temporary events may not be reduced to the conditions of their existence, and so the book also searches for the creative potentials of temporary urbanism, which are found in questioning, experimenting and innovating.

Temporary urbanism, as a pattern of events, is analysed at the intersection of three forms of temporality: instrumental, existential and experimental. Instrumental temporality is characterized by a utilitarian approach to time, accelerating quantified time for higher productivity and profitability. Existential temporality reflects the intuitive understanding of temporality, the materiality of the city which mediates this temporality, and the vulnerability and precariousness of the social and natural worlds in the face of globalization.

Experimental temporality, meanwhile, is the view to the future, drawing on events as spaces of questioning, experimenting and innovating. The theoretical analysis draws on insights from the fields of philosophy, social sciences, and architectural and urban cultural history and theory. The investigation also draws on empirical material from the practices of architecture, urban design and planning, with a particular focus on the manifestations of time in the city and the experiences of temporary urbanism.

This investigation is an analysis of a social trend and its spatial implications. In undertaking this analysis, it is important to engage with the philosophical concepts of time. Thinking about time and temporality has been a long-standing preoccupation of all schools of thought, and therefore it is essential to benefit from this enormous heritage. The analysis, however, cannot rely solely on philosophical concepts and analyses, as these concepts need to be mediated through social processes and material changes to become visible in concrete experiences of a society. Many philosophical concepts focus on the metaphysical aspects of time and the intuitive sense of temporality. Time and space, after all, are in many respects metaphysical concepts, as they do not exist as such but are concepts that are developed to account for aspects of reality. While these concepts are the basic building blocks of individual experience, and they are fundamental to our analysis, we need to be able to translate them into the analysis of the emergence of a social trend and the transformation of the urban space. Social practices unfold and are shaped through their material and institutional dimensions. The gap between the intelligible and the sensible, therefore, needs to be bridged by social and spatial practice. In other words, it is through social processes, spatial transformation and the personal engagement that the sensible is experienced and the intelligible is constructed.

Structure of the book

The book is organized in three parts, which dialectically show the overall causes and consequences of temporary urbanism: instrumental processes accelerate time and generate temporariness, existential processes show precarity, adjustment and resistance, while creative processes look for a way forward.

The first part examines instrumental temporality; its two chapters analyse the concepts of time and locate the conditions of temporary urbanism in a broader context: how time has become treated as an instrument and an asset, how it has been subject to the pressures of acceleration in the process of globalization and how transience and ephemerality are the outcome of these pressures. Chapter 2 analyses the institutional and instrumental concepts of time, which have been developed to grapple with ephemerality and change. It argues that the concepts of time, while rooted in biological rhythms, are social constructions. Time has been conceptualized to regulate events and instigate a sense of order, while abstraction and institutionalization have paved the way for envisaging time as an instrument, equating it with monetary value and productivity outcome, with dramatic consequences for how the city is organized. The chapter is organized in four sections: the theories, technologies and institutions that have been developed to regulate temporality, and their implications for space. It analyses how time is reified through philosophical concepts and scientific theories; how it is captured and measured through changing technologies; and how it is framed through habits, institutions and law. The impact of these developments on urban space is the first basis for investigating temporary urbanism.

Chapter 3 investigates the accelerated beats of global time: how the city's rhythms are created and managed, and how technological and economic change has accelerated these rhythms, creating a sense of restlessness and ephemerality. In exploring the methods of mobility and organizing work, the significance of technological and economic changes in how time is envisaged and managed in the city becomes evident. The processes of reification, quantification and commodification have paved the way for an instrumental treatment of temporality, turning it increasingly into the subject of market pressures for speed, productivity and profit maximization. The chapter starts with an analysis of innovation and its role in urban transformation, followed by five sections on the social implications of technical and economic change: expanding time and space, filling the gaps, nomadic urbanity, radical simultaneity and illusions of immateriality, and disrupted institutions. This shows how adjustment to the accelerated beats of globalization has become an existential condition.

The second part focuses on existential temporality; its two chapters show the intuitive sense of temporality as an existential condition, and how the processes of instrumentalization and acceleration of time have had an impact on this temporality, generating anxiety and fragmentation. Chapter 4 addresses temporality, memory and identity. The chapter explores the personal sense of time and its complex relationship with instrumental notions of time. It examines the existential unfolding of time at the intersection of phenomenological temporality, memory and identity. The main argument is that subjectivity, memory and identity are the key features of existential temporality, and that their disruption or loss leads to cultural amnesia, a sense of transience, loss of collective memory, and fluidity and multiplicity in the common frameworks of meaning and identity. While a sense of continuity and a hope for psychological security may persist in many traces, the intuitive temporality itself is not a continuous fabric, as it is subject to the fragmentation of selves and events.

The chapter is organized in four parts: inner phenomenological time, memory and the reconstructed time, identity and the narrated time, and the multiplicity of the selves and voices that experience and narrate temporal multiplicity.

In Chapter 5, the focus is on the linkages made to the natural environment and the results of the ruptures in these linkages. It is organized in six parts. It first introduces the paradoxical approaches to nature in the modern period, and the way nature has been understood within the human body and in the wider natural world, both showing a dichotomous and ambiguous relationship. The natural world within the human body has been split into a mind–body distinction, while the natural world around us has been turned first into a subject of conquest and then to one of concern. The state of nature as a state of apparent originality refers to a nostalgic memory of the time that humans lived in apparent harmony with the natural world, while the absence of this harmony and the fragility of the natural world are vividly experienced today. The result is a sense of contingency and anxiety about the future, which is exacerbated by temporal acceleration.

After investigating the instrumental construction of time and its largely problematic impacts on the existential dimensions of society and nature, the third part focuses on experimental temporality, looking for the creative potentials of temporary urbanism and their implications for the future of the city. Chapter 6 concentrates on events and prospects, addressing experimental temporality as both diverse and future oriented, and how temporary interventions may act as catalysts for change. It investigates the creative potentials of temporary urbanism in three broad sections: questioning, experimenting and innovating. It examines how temporary urbanism questions the status quo through displacement and the break-up of structures, which change perspectives and indicate structural change, experimenting through how it contributes to the creation of times and spaces of possibility, in particular the opportune times and the public space, and innovating through how it can be significant in the processes of making space, in particular through the involvement of civil society forces in alternative practices. While Chapter 3 examined innovation in technical and economic terms and its contribution to temporal acceleration, this chapter identifies the innovative and creative potentials of temporary urbanism in areas beyond economic considerations, without losing sight of its possible shortcomings.

Some of the key themes of the book on the implications of ephemerality for the future of cities are brought together in Chapter 7, which concludes the book. It is organized in two sections. The first section addresses the three broad concepts of time: substantive, relational and intuitive. The three sides of time are all at work to construct the meaning of temporality, with many tensions and contradictions that emerge in their interface, with different impacts of ephemerality and temporal acceleration on the visions of the future.

Temporariness has a wide variety of meanings, some or all of which may be at work in any particular situation. In the second section, different processes of temporariness are summarized as embedded, intentional and experiential. The interplay between the potentials for stimulating creativity and/or generating precarity, especially in the context of social and environmental vulnerability, becomes significant.

PART ONE

Instrumental Temporality

The two chapters in this part analyse the concepts of time and locate the conditions of temporary urbanism in a broader context: how time has become treated as an instrument and an asset, how it has been subject to the pressures of acceleration in the process of globalization and how transience is the outcome of these pressures.

2

Regulating Change, Reifying Time

Temporary urbanism is based on events that seem to be random, outside the normal rhythm of things, disrupting the settled habits of society and disregarding the routines that regulate everyday life. As such, these events seem to be a challenge to the structured sense of time that is the hallmark of normalcy, what holds society together. This chapter analyses the institutional and instrumental concepts of time, and how they have been developed to grapple with ephemerality and change. It argues that, while living organisms live through a biological rhythm, the concepts of time are social constructions, which need to be understood in the context of their social circumstances (Lefebvre, 1991; Adam, 1995). Time has been conceptualized to regulate events and incorporate a sense of philosophical and social order into time, and abstraction and institutionalization have paved the way for envisaging time as an instrument, equating it with monetary value and productivity outcome, with dramatic consequences for how the city is organized.

The chapter is organized in four sections: the theories, technologies and institutions that have been developed to regulate temporality, and their implications for space. We see how time is reified through philosophical concepts and scientific theories; how it is captured and measured through changing technologies; and how it is framed through habits, institutions and law. The impact of these developments on urban space is the first basis for investigating temporary urbanism. This analysis is developed in examining the concept of time, its nature and structure, and its close association with change; how time is measured and accounted for; how time is institutionalized through social beliefs and practices; and how time is made permanent through being located in space. Together they show how change is tamed and managed, and how temporary urbanism as an expression of change may be a challenge to this settled pattern of thinking and managing time.

Reifying time

Temporary urbanism may be partly interpreted as an intensification of change and a departure from predictable routines. A long historical process has been at work to institute a concept of change that would manage change and limit the extent of vulnerability to change. It led to understanding time as a measure of change, conceptualized either as an independent substance or a set of relationships that need to be shaped and tamed.

The nature of time: Relation between events

A fundamental question about the nature of time, which has recurred throughout the ages, is whether time exists at all. Those who have given a positive answer to this question have conceptualized time as an independent substance, while those who have doubted the existence of this substance have thought of time as a relationship. This relationship, furthermore, has been conceptualized as one between phenomena or between the observer and the phenomena. This conceptualization of time runs parallel to the conceptualization of space, with direct implications for how social institutions are developed and how the spaces of the city are organized and used.

The substantive, absolute or abstract, view of time thinks of time as an independent substance. According to this view, called Platonism or absolutism with respect to time, which was held by Plato, Newton and others, time is thought to be 'like an empty container into which things and events may be placed; but it is a container that exists independently of what (if anything) is placed in it' (Markosian, 2014). For Plato (1977:37), time was created together with the universe and it was 'a moving image of eternity'; day and night, months and years were parts of time, while past and future were forms of time (Plato, 1977:51). Descartes also held an abstract view of time, held to be 'a generalized abstraction from the "durations" of particular bodies' (Slowik, 2014). Isaac Newton used the substantive concept of time to develop a complete system of physics. For Newton, writing in 1687, 'Absolute, true and mathematical time, of itself, and from its own nature flows equably without regard to anything external, and by another name is called duration' (Newton, Principia, quoted in Whitrow, 1972:100). Newtonian mechanics, based on his concepts of time, space and motion, dominated the modern science for three centuries until the arrival of the theory of relativity in the early twentieth century. However, as an entity that cannot be seen, touched or captured, thinking of time as a continuous substance requires metaphysical assumptions. Thinking of it as a continuous flow may appear as a metaphorical device to come to terms with what may be too abstract to experience. Before the arrival of philosophical and scientific theories of abstract time, temporality could be depicted by a god who was in charge of events, changing the course of time in response to circumstances, but ultimately representing a distinction and dialogue between the physical and the metaphysical.

An alternative view interpreted time as a relationship between phenomena, rather than existing as an entity. This view, held by Aristotle and others (including, especially, Leibniz), argued that time does not exist independently of the events that occur in time. This view is typically called either Reductionism or Relationism with Respect to Time, since according to this view, all talk that appears to be about time can somehow be reduced to talk about temporal relations among things and events (Markosian, 2014). Aristotle (*Physics*, Book IV, 10) was aware of the difficulties of proving the existence of time, as it was made up of parts which did not exist: the past ('it has happened and does not exist'), the future ('does not yet exist') and the now ('which is not a part of time') that links and separates the past from the future ('it is not easy to see whether it always stays the same or whether it is always different') (Aristotle, 1996:102–3). For him, time was closely related to motion and change, not as an independent reality but as a measure of this change. Despite questioning the substantive nature of time, however, he held it to be continuous, a reflection of the sequence of before and after: 'time is a number of change in respect of before and after; and because it is a number of something continuous, it is continuous itself' (Aristotle, 1996:108).

In the modern period, the critique of substantive time was advocated by Leibniz in his argument against Newton. Leibniz rejected the notion of moments as abstract concepts and instead argued for the significance of events. Rather than a thing in itself, time was the order of events, in the same way that space was an order of coexistence rather than an independent entity. Leibniz, however, did not believe in the randomness or relativity of these relations (Leibniz, 1979:89). His grand principle was that everything has a reason, and therefore these relations could be explained in functional and calculable terms. 'Precisely this is my Grand principle ... that nothing happens without a reason that one can always render as to why the matter has run its course this way rather than that' (quoted in Heidegger, 1996:119). This principle, as Heidegger (1996:120) interpreted it, meant 'that every thing counts as existing when and only when it has been securely established as a calculable object for cognition'. He argued that this principle, which has been in the making for a long time, has shaped the centre of Western modernity, as it determines all cognition and behaviour (Heidegger, 1996:121). When applied to temporality, it produces an instrumental understanding of time, turning it into a calculable and functional phenomenon.

In principle, Leibniz agreed with Newton that time was frame independent. However, the frame-independent notions of simultaneity and duration that had defined the concepts of space and time were abandoned with the arrival of Einstein's general and special theories of relativity, which showed how time and space were relative, dependent on the observer (Audi, 1995:805). Time could not be conceptualized in isolation from the frames in which it was being experienced (Whitrow, 1972:106–7). Comparing two clocks, one moving and the other at rest, showed how the moving clock would run faster, proving that time was relative to the observers rather than existing as an absolute entity. This relationship, however, is not completely free of fixed frames of reference, such as the speed of light. As Whitrow (1972:116) puts it, 'whereas for Newton time was independent of the universe and for Leibniz it was an aspect of the universe, Einstein's theory leads us to regard it as an aspect of the relationship between the universe and the observer'. The theory of relativity introduces yet another level of fluidity into the concept of time, turning it into an observer-dependent phenomenon. Temporariness becomes an interpretation from an observer's perspective. What is permanent to one observer may appear to be temporary to another. Different perspectives will have different interpretations of temporality.

Different concepts of time aim to regulate the occurrence of events into an overall framework which could be discovered, explained and managed. For the substantive view of time, events are different manifestations of an underlying substance, following the universal rules embedded in this substance. An event is the empirical manifestation of a metaphysical ideal type, a mere instance of a general substance. They do not unsettle the eternal concept of time as it exists above the everyday phenomena. Compared to the general, eternal and abstract concept of time, all events are temporary and particular. For the relational view, however, time does not exist as such and its order is not universal and pre-existing, but it is an expression of the relations between events and their circumstances. Relations between events would determine their interpretation as temporary or permanent. Temporariness becomes a matter of interpretation of, and the character of the relations between, events. What matters more here are the events. But even in this relational way of thinking about time, the concept of time is still a unitary one. It is a single concept whose nature is substantive or relational. A more radical interpretation of relationality would abandon the idea of time altogether, as what is being discussed is not an abstraction called time but various forms of relations, which can be called by many different names.

As we will see in the following chapters, the reified and instrumental idea of time prevails in regulating the process of urban life, and it is always challenged by the relational idea of time, as time is experienced through this relationship between the phenomena, and between the observer and the world.

The structure of time: Linking sequential fragments

In addition to the nature of time, another fundamental question is about how time is structured: what is the relationship between past, present and future, and whether time is linear or cyclical, continuous or fragmented.

It has been argued that the most important question about time is its passage: whether it passes or it is a series of events that our mind represents in a sequence of past, present and future (Le Poidevin, 2007). It is the dispute between the substantive and the relational concepts of time that is reflected in the way time is structured. For some, meanwhile, this sequential structure collapses when viewed from personal experience and memory. T.S. Eliot, for example, starts his poem Four Quartets by the idea that all time is eternally present, and how past, present and future are embedded in each other.

The cyclical idea of time is rooted in the circadian time embedded in the biorhythms of life forms and natural processes. It is based on a repetitive regularity in the natural world: living organisms' biological patterns such as the rhythms of breathing and heartbeat, their cycles of birth and death, as well as in the planetary pulses that generate a repetitive pattern of day and night, months, seasons and years. It is 'a continuous sequence of events with neither beginning nor end, the past forever repeating itself' (Aveni, 2000:327) (Figure 2.1). Nicolas Poussin's seventeenth-century painting *A Dance to the Music of Time*, which became the source of inspiration for Anthony Powell's novels of the same name, shows a circle of dancers dancing to the lyre music played by an old angel, displaying the cyclical and somewhat inevitable rhythm of life. In most cultures, these cyclical beats are celebrated through rituals and regular events, which mark another turn of a cycle, as a sign of a cosmic order that constrains unwelcome events, manages time and generates a sense of continuity and security. The concept of reincarnation is one of the many ways that the cyclical way of thinking about time tries to capture a larger form of time.

Through cultural practices, a common sense, cyclical concept in biological life is extended to human societies as a whole, observed in the succession of kings, recurrence of floods and earthquakes, emergence and decline of cities, rise and fall of civilizations, and birth and death of the universe. In these accounts, biological, social and historical concepts of time are intertwined with geological and cosmological time to construct a narrative of how time unfolds in cycles. Cyclical temporality helps predict the future, as it is likely to be an iteration of the past, offering a sense of security and familiarity, with a conservative and protective attitude that would avoid the risks posed by the unknown. Temporary events make sense only in a general framework of recurrence, and as such they are disciplined to find symbolic meaning and a place in a temporal order.

FIGURE 2.1 *Observing and experiencing the natural rhythms are at the heart of the concepts of time (Colombo, Sri Lanka).*

In contrast to the cyclical notion of time, a linear concept characterizes the modern attitude to time, associated with cause and effect, belief in evolution and progress, and a hopeful outlook to a future that will be better than the past. It is in contrast to the fatalism of cyclical thinking: the future would no longer mimic the past and there is no fear of being trapped in the inevitable turns of the wheels of time. Thinking of time as an independent, homogeneous and continuous entity was closely related to the concepts of duration and flow, and the structure of time as linear, unfolding from the past to present and the future. Linear time was present in some ancient cultures who believed in the victory of good over evil and a progressive idea of history, but by the medieval period the dominant mood was in favour of cyclical time. The invention of mechanical clocks, scientific discoveries, exploration and conquest of the world, and the money economy revived the idea of progressive history in the West after the Renaissance. In 1638, Galileo represented time as a geometrical straight line (Whitrow, 1972:98). Three years after Newton wrote about the flow of time, John Locke wrote, 'Duration is but as it were the length of one straight line *in infinitum*, not capable of multiplicity, variation or figure, but is one common measure of all existence whatever, wherein all things, whilst they exist, equally partake' (quoted in Whitrow, 1972:101). It is indeed these concepts of time that are still widely held today. According to the *Oxford English Dictionary*, the many meanings of the word 'time', which is one of the 1000 most frequently used words in the language, start with its most general and philosophical one: 'The indefinite continued progress of existence and events in the past, present, and future regarded as a whole'.

What gave a strong momentum to the linear concept of time was Darwin's theory of evolution, which showed continuous change in new directions, rather than a return to earlier forms. Similarly, the Big Bang theory identifies a linear concept of time: a clear beginning and direction for time that was triggered when the whole universe came into being and started to evolve (Hawking, 1988). Even today, however, some cosmologists theorize about the possibility of cyclical time, in which the Big Bang was preceded by previous universes and many will follow after the demise of this universe (Aveni, 2000:329). Meanwhile, the second law of thermodynamics reveals the inherent entropy of the universe: the growing loss of energy that would lead to decline and disorder. Cyclical time also lives on in economic cycles, which in different sizes and scales, from the short business cycles to long Kondratieff waves, mark the beats of global capitalism. But they are all seen to be part of an overall linear movement, in which the arrow of time moves forward and growth is apparently inevitable.

A direct implication of the notion of linear time and its association with progress is a negative attitude to the past. Hegel, and following him Marx, believed in a progressive march of history, one period replacing another towards a more complex, and ultimately perfect, outcome (Marx and Engels, 1968; Taylor, 1979). The social sciences continually compared the modern society with its predecessors, which they found to be underdeveloped (Durkheim, 1972b). The past was no longer held as a possible model for the future, as it had been in the cyclical notions of time. The past was a less developed state, where organization and technology were in a more primitive stage, whereas the future was believed to be inevitably more complex and more advanced than before. People and places that embodied the past habits and ways of life were considered to be inferior and outdated, confronted with a stark choice: either to modernize or to disappear, both of which involved abandoning what was left from the past. This optimistic belief in the future, however, was shaken by world wars and repeated periods of economic stagnation, the failure of the utopian experiments in revolutionary change and the global environmental crisis that was linked with the industrial civilization. Optimism gave its place to a mood in which the progressive character of linear time was no longer guaranteed, and the future became uncertain.

In the cyclical notion of time, temporary events are part of a recurring pattern, taken to be a part of the nature of the world. In the linear idea, events may be judged according to their contribution to progress or decline, as following the rules or as being mere anomalies. The temporal order is aligned with progress and optimism, so temporary events could be seen as the possible signs of change in the direction of progress, or as the early signs of decay and disorder. Both interpretations of time as linear or cyclical are attempts at constructing a temporal structure through a clear narrative, with which the apparently random events can be tamed within a logical framework that is easy to understand. It is a framework that is described in geometrical, spatial images: cycles and lines. The use of mathematics to describe the world is a fundamental feature of the scientific attitude, giving a reducible and comprehensible shape to a vast array of complex phenomena that constitute the world.

Time, however, could equally be interpreted as the overall pattern of fragmented and discontinuous events that unfold in a polyrhythmic manner. What gives coherence to this heterogeneous and disjointed series of events are our interpretations, anthropological and phenomenological. Temporal coherence comes from either a structure imposed on them through institutional arrangements, or connected together through personal experience and memory, as we will explore in the following chapters. Disjointed events are linked together through a sequential structure of past–present–future and are imagined to be moving in progressive directions or repeating themselves. To generate this sense of order, a sophisticated system of measurement is created that can account for change and support the instrumental conceptualization of time.

Measuring time

Quantifying time is a method of accounting for change and for translating an abstract concept into an empirical existence. Conceptualizing time and change are closely intertwined, and the methods of measuring time have been increasingly more accurate, systematized and universalized, finding physical expression in many timekeeping devices. Measuring and objectifying time is the way in which a theoretical idea finds practical application, a bridge from *episteme* to *phronesis* through *techne*.

Time as the measure of change

Observing change in the natural world and devising ways of coping with this change can be detected in many cultures, going back deep into the history of human societies. The Greek philosopher Heraclitus, who lived at the end of the sixth century BC, is well known for his philosophy of flow and change. Heraclitus is quoted by Socrates (in *Cratylus*, 402a) to have said that 'all things are in motion and nothing at rest; he compares them to the stream of a river, and says that you cannot go into the same water twice' (Plato, 1982:439). At the same time, Heraclitus believed in a rational, divine order for the cosmos, which was possible, though difficult, to be discovered by humans (Curd, 2012).

Continual change is also the basis on which Buddha, who lived around the same time in India, developed his philosophy of emancipation from time: humans are caught in a recurring cycle of change, which can be painful, as he observed in ageing, disease and death; but it was possible to overcome this painful cycle through self-awareness and search for enlightenment, which offered a path to freedom from the cycle of life and a place in eternity (Rahula, 1974; Gethin, 1998; Gowans, 2003) (Figure 2.2). Many belief systems that have emerged in different cultures have linked the ephemerality of life on earth to a spiritual eternity beyond this world, either in the form of gods and angels who live for ever but somewhere not far from mortal humans or in the form of an eternal human soul that departs at the end of the body's life but lives on forever. Although widely different philosophies and beliefs, they all indicate a recognition of change as the fundamental feature of the natural world, which includes humans, and the search for ideas and practices that can help deal with our exposure to this never-ending and apparently inevitable

FIGURE 2.2 *Many systems of thought have been devised for managing change. An example is Buddhism, where the ultimate goal is stopping the painful cycle of return (Colombo, Sri Lanka).*

change. The search for fixed points and unchanging orders has been the human societies' attempts for coming to terms with, and overcoming, our vulnerabilities towards change.

Time is the window through which we can observe and conceptualize change. Time in itself is an abstract concept; it cannot be directly grasped by our senses, but by constructing an idea through observing the material changes that take place in us and in the world around us, we think of time as the sum total of these changes. As Aristotle (1996:105) argues, 'time is not change, but ... it does not exist without change'. For him, time and change are interdependent: 'Time is a measure of change and of being changed' (1996:109), it is 'a number of change in respect of before and after' (Aristotle, 1996:106). The ancient Greeks used the word *Chronos* to refer to this notion of time as a measurable phenomenon. Reified, sequential and quantified time is accounted for, and controlled by, numbers. By conceptualizing time as measure, the questions that are asked are about 'the quantity of duration, the length of periodicity, the age of an object or artifact and the rate of acceleration of bodies whether on the surface of the earth or in the firmament beyond' (Smith, 1986:4). Quantified time measures an abstract substance and provides a framework within which events can be located and managed. It covers all temporal scales and speeds of change: from biological rhythms to social, historical, geological and cosmological ones, all integrated into a hierarchical system of measurement ruled by mathematics. In this way, all events, short term or long, are accounted for within a linear and measurable structure, which locates them and defines them. It describes when an event occurred and how long it lasted, therefore helps determining the social and historical context.

Four historical trends in timekeeping

If time is thought to be the measure of change, the ways in which this measurement has been developed and used become significant. Assigning numerical value to time is the first fundamental step in the process of quantification. Following this step, at least four long historical trends can be observed that show how this process of measuring time has evolved: precision, systematization, materialization and collectivization. Through these trends, time has been measured ever more precisely; with the help of and projection onto material objects; standardized, systematized and universalized through social institutions and conventions; and employed to manage and regulate the beats of everyday life.

The quest for precision in timekeeping is traceable through changes in the bases of calculation and advances in technology. A major transition in timekeeping has been from observing natural phenomena to developing social conventions measured by mathematical calculations. Like plants and animals, humans have always been sensitive to the changes in the natural cycles such as days, months, seasons and years. The quest for precision started alongside the emergence of agriculture and the development of human settlements, when sensitivity to environmental change was more crucial for the settled farmers than it had been for the hunters and gatherers before them. Precise time measurement started, for a mixture of symbolic and practical reasons, with the ancient Mesopotamians, who also invented writing, reasoning and religion (Bottéro, 2000). The Babylonian arithmetic was based on the number 60, which was used to subdivide a circle into 360 degrees, and the day and night into 6 equal parts, paving the way for our system of 24 hours. The pursuit of precision, however, was limited to astronomy, rather than finding expression in everyday social life. Priests and astronomers in Mesopotamia and Egypt divided the night into twelve equal parts, which was followed by the same division for the day. As the periods of light and darkness differed, however, these were 'unequal hours', which were used for everyday purposes (Aveni, 2000). Adopted by the Romans, unequal hours were used in Europe until the invention of mechanical clocks in the Middle Ages, and in Japan even until 1870 (Hellyer, 1974).

The quest for precision has also been grounded in the technological advances that have made timekeeping ever more detailed and precise, changing its unit from days and hours to seconds. Although sundials had been used for centuries, the mechanical clocks shifted the basis of timekeeping from environmental observation to mechanical methods. Timekeeping has eventually transformed its foundation from planetary movements to the subatomic world. In 1956, a system called Ephemeris time was introduced, redefining the basis of time measurement in terms of the annual motion of the earth around the sun. The unit of time was a second, calculated as 1/86,400 of the mean solar day (Bell and Goldman, 1986:5–6). However, the irregularities in the rotation of the earth made this calculation unreliable in determining the exact definition of the mean solar day. Atomic clocks were then used to overcome this problem and offer a more reliable definition for the second, which is still in use to this day. In 1964, the definition of a second was changed to the time that an electron takes to pass from one energy state to another (Aveni, 2000:99). As defined by the International System of Units (SI), the second is, 'the duration of 9,192,631 periods of radiation corresponding to the transition between the two hyperfine levels of ground state of the caesium 133 atom' (Bell and Goldman, 1986:6).

The second trend is the systematization and standardization of time and the production of a universal time across the globe. As railways linked different towns and cities to each other, it became obvious that each place had its own local time, which was not aligned with others. London and Cornwall, for example, had a time difference of twenty minutes. For the trains to operate, however, their times needed to be coordinated and standardized. Navigation around the globe for trade or conquest had already established the standard of Greenwich Mean Time, which was extended to the railways in 1880 in an act of Parliament that recognized the 'railway time' (Figure 2.3). This coordination was also needed between countries, so four years later, an international standard was set for time zones on the basis of Greenwich Mean Time (or Universal Time). It standardized the global space and time, so that one

FIGURE 2.3 *Railways linked cities together and created the need and the necessary infrastructure for the integration of different local times into a shared system (Newark, UK).*

hour corresponded to fifteen degrees of longitude (Hellyer, 1974:12–13). The establishment of the universal time was possible on the basis of the might and global reach of the British navy. Now the US Navy's Time Service Department is the official source of time for the Department of Defence, the standard of time across the United States and the Global Positioning System which is used across the world (Time Service Department, 2014). Systematization and standardization of global time, therefore, have been based on the increased mobility and connectivity between different locales, as well as the presence of national and global powers, and international agreements, which could envisage and enforce universal standards.

The third historical trend is the materialization of timekeeping through the objects that have been used to measure time. With the reification of time, there has been a trend of objectification of timekeeping, in which increasingly more sophisticated devices have been developed and used. Rather than observing the changing natural phenomena, which has been the main way of keeping time for most of human history, we need devices that tell us precisely where we stand in the universal time. From a time in which only a few sundials, water clocks and clock towers existed in a town, industrial and digital technology has made the large-scale production of clocks, watches and other timekeeping devices possible. These devices are all part of an interconnected network of timekeeping that relies on some key points of reference. In one of its routine calculations, in October 2014, the US Naval Observatory used forty-eight weighted atomic clocks to calculate its mean time, which is used as a point of reference for many other forms of time measurement (Time Service Department, 2014).

The fourth historical trend is the externalization and collectivization of timekeeping through public display and personal ownership of these material objects and the organization of space. Together they constitute a public infrastructure that regulates social life (Madanipour, 2007). In many ways, the work of architecture is a fundamental part of the processes of objectifying and externalizing time. On the one hand, as solid structures they partially compensate for the exposure to change in the environment. With buildings, we are able to cope with the cycles of day and night, seasons and years. At the same time, they are structures of temporality, in the sense that they regulate our patterns of life. The order of rooms inside a building, and the order of buildings and open spaces across the city are not directly timekeeping devices but make a significant contribution to the construction of social temporality and the organization of time in the city. Design is an integral part of the processes of temporal ordering, setting up explicit and implicit frameworks for human behaviour.

Sundials were the most important form of public timekeeping in the ancient world, which is why they were on display in Greek and Roman public places (Vitruvius, 1999). In some cities, timekeeping was displayed through specific buildings. In Rome's Forum, noon was marked by the passage of the sun between two prominent buildings, the Rostrum and the Grecostasis, and was announced by a timekeeper. In Beijing, a sundial in front of the imperial palace was a standard for timekeeping and a symbol for the power of the emperor (the son of heaven) over time (Figure 2.4). In Tenochtitlan, the capital of the Aztecs (current Mexico city), the opening and the closing of the market, the times of prayer and other important events were announced

FIGURE 2.4 *A sundial in front of the imperial palace symbolizes the supreme power of the emperor, the 'son of heaven', over time (Beijing, China).*

from a round temple in the plaza in front of the great Temple Mayor (Aveni, 2000:92). In medieval Christian and Muslim towns, the church bell tower and the mosque's minaret kept the time by announcing the prayer times, ordering urban lives and facilitating navigation in the urban space. Clock towers offered more precision and went beyond religious routines, helping to regulate the life of the town as a place of trade and exchange (Saalman, 1968; Aveni, 2000) (Figure 2.5). Together, these public displays of timekeeping, which grew ever

FIGURE 2.5 *Mechanical clocks changed the concept of time and the methods of its measurement, becoming part of a public infrastructure of quantitative time (Prague, Czech Republic).*

more precise and ubiquitous, dominated the landscape. If, as John Locke (quoted in Whitrow, 1972:101) wrote in 1690, 'Duration ... is one common measure of all existence whatever', it was increasingly important for the modern city to capture and display this common measure.

With the changing technologies of measuring time, and the penetration of timekeeping deeper into various aspects of life, the number of these devices has increased to the extent that they are present everywhere in the public and private life. They are installed on walls and building facades, finding the pride of place on the mantelpiece in the house, and to a situation that almost everyone now carries a timekeeping device in the form of calendars, diaries, watches, mobile phones and computers, and in case they do not do so they are continuously reminded of time by the radio and television, and in every transaction and every passage through the city. Quantitative time, therefore, has taken material shape through these timekeeping devices and material reflections in many more objects and practices which are found everywhere. Their ubiquitous presence everywhere signals the undeniable triumph of quantitative time in modern urban life.

The subdivision of day into hours, minutes and seconds was a mathematical interpretation of the routine changes in the environment, an invention that superimposed a human convention onto a series of natural phenomena, connecting them through a temporal sequence. This marriage of numbers and events initiated a tension between biological rhythms and mathematical calculations, between the ways of our bodies and environments on the one hand, and our concepts and social conventions on the other hand, between events and laws. The invention of mechanical clocks paved the way for the emergence of an abstract notion of time and a mechanistic concept of nature, as exemplified by Kepler who thought of universe as a clock. As Lewis Mumford argues, mechanical clocks 'dissociated time from human events and helped create the belief in an independent world of science' (quoted in Whitrow, 1972:21). By now, atomic clocks and digital networks have helped create a universal sense of time that envisages the entire world as a sphere of simultaneity ruled by numbers.

Institutionalizing time

The concept of time is a social institution for understanding and managing change. Time and the social and physical infrastructure that manifest and support it constitute an overall framework of meaning. Continual change is a fundamental feature of the natural and the social world, and to be able to cope with this change, human societies have developed cultural instruments that would help them feel in control. Faced with the reality of being exposed to powerful forces beyond our control, narratives have been developed to make sense of these forces, and tools to conceptualize and measure change. To understand and control the scale and pace of change that we observe in our bodies and in the world around us, a series of ideas and practices have been instituted that would link together the incidents of change in a meaningful way. The concept of time is one of these cultural instruments: it is developed to explain change and help manage it, and as such it is embedded in almost all ideas and practices: in beliefs, rituals and myths; in art, science and technology; as well as in everyday practices. While change may be the occurrence of events and their impact on the world, time is the narrative that makes sense of these events by placing them into an overarching framework, turning them into episodes in a line rather than random happenings without precedence or consequence. It is a concept that seeks, and injects a sense of, regularity in phenomena.

This is a process that expresses a desire to overcome, or at best tame, ephemerality by framing, measuring and regulating temporality. The future that unfolds through the passage of time gives us a sense of the unknown that plays an important role in the construction of our individual and collective subjectivity, in which fear and hope are intertwined. Regulating time shows a desire to deal with the continual process of change and the apparent randomness of events, seeking a permanent logic of temporality through science, technology and law. Any irregularity is expected to be either explained (through philosophy, religion and science), tamed (through technology) and managed (through habits, institutions and laws). Together, they form some of the fundamental pillars of the cultural order that may offer a sense of security and continuity to human society. Random events, however, always occur, posing a challenge to these frameworks of regularizing temporality.

Social institutions, as Emile Durkheim (1972c:71) defined them, are 'all the beliefs and modes of conduct instituted by the collectivity'. Durkheim aimed to show how social institutions were the substance of social life, existing prior to and acting as a framework for individual beliefs and conducts. These institutions constitute a social fabric into which individuals are born and within which their mentalities and behaviour are shaped. They are not easy to change by an individual and so their impact on the individual mentality and conduct would be constitutive and regulatory. If the individual behaviour does not comply with these social institutions, it is considered to be transgressive and may be frowned upon or even punished.

In everyday language, social institutions refer to a range of social forms such as family, sport and religion. In everyday usage, they may also refer to particular forms of organization such as school, police and government. In more precise sociological definitions, social institutions are 'regular patterns of behaviour' and 'an ensemble of social roles'; norms and sanctions regulate them and individuals are socialized into them (Turner, 2006:300). In his analysis of social systems, Talcott Parsons (1952:39) defined institutions as 'a complex of institutionalized role integrates': an institution was a unit of social structure formed by 'a plurality of interdependent role-patterns or components of them'. Social institutions were a mechanism of social control, which is developed to confront social deviance (Parsons, 1952:297ff). On the basis of this functionalist analysis, these roles, and the rules and customs that enforce them, are thought to have 'given objectives' (Wells, 1970:7). Conventional approaches in mainstream sociology would therefore identify five clusters of institutions in society: economic (production, distribution and consumption of goods and services); political (regulation and access to power); stratificational (prestige and social status); familial (kinship, marriage and family, regulating reproduction); and cultural (religious and symbolic) institutions (Turner, 2006:300).

From our vantage point, however, we may see that as societies have grown larger, more complex and more diverse, it has become ever more difficult to identify a clear set of collective beliefs and actions, as it may have been in the past. As the social attitudes have become more fluid and multidimensional, the diversity and plurality of ideas and practices have become inevitable features of society. Furthermore, social institutions should not be seen as objects; they are indeed social processes that are reproduced and therefore subject to change and difference. The continued existence of social institutions depends on the individual acceptance and re-enactment of these collective ideas and practices (Searle, 1995; Bourdieu, 2000). Therefore, if large enough numbers abandon a particular way of thinking or behaving, it would disappear; after all, social institutions are not static, and they do change over time. As analysts such as Michel Foucault (2001, 2002) have shown, social institutions may reproduce unjust relations, which would need to be opened up to critical scrutiny, rather than accepted as delivering a desirable equilibrium in a social system. Moreover, the analysis of social institutions may tend to see order and regularity in what may in practice be no more than a disorganized reality.

Social institutions are the manifestations of social order, as well as the mechanisms to ensure that this social order is instituted and maintained. Social institutions are at the heart of the continuous process of creating social structures, in which individual behaviour and random events are brought into an institutional framework, with the aim of understanding, harnessing and regulating them. Anything that stands outside this framework may then be called an abnormality, a deviance. A key instrument in the construction of social institutions is the regularization of beliefs and behaviours, or repetition and routinization. The role of social institutions is to generate recurring patterns and persistent forms of belief and behaviour; in doing so they maintain a sense of safety and familiarity and confront the threat of randomness and disorder. This shows how the management of temporality is the primary ingredient of social institutions and social structures: they generate norms and routines and expect conformity with these norms. The temporal order and its regularity offer the possibility of continuity, predictability and avoidance of unforeseen change. This process of ordering can be seen in most parts of society.

The tension between the permanent and the temporary penetrates all spheres of life. An example is the realm of the household, and the conventions and practices that have shaped around it. A long historical process has led to the formation of family as a unit of social reproduction, supported by its laws and conventions, which are particular to each society and culture. As a social institution, family is a framework through which sexual relationships and demographic reproduction through time are managed, as a cornerstone of social order. The formation of temporary households in the modern period could therefore be considered a threat, undermining age-old ideas and practices. However, as the temporary arrangements have spread, they have become a new norm, accepted by many as a common social practice. The existing social institutions are replaced with a more flexible one; in turn these new arrangements have become so common as to be considered a social institution which is increasingly protected by laws and cultures.

The conquest of time and change through social institutions can be traced through the arts, myths and legends, where change and its emotional impact are expressed and explained: through routines and traditions, where beliefs and practices are reproduced through repetition and intergenerational transfer; through organizational forms such as family, cultural conventions and religion, where these beliefs and practices are regulated and controlled; and through government and law, where these practices are clearly bounded and controlled. They seem to be all arrangements for establishing and welcoming some phenomena as familiar, permanent and variations on a theme, while rejecting or limiting what is considered to be unfamiliar and out of tune.

Thinking of time as an independent substance or a relationship, envisaging it through mathematical formulae and geometrical shapes, regular patterns and functional purposes, shows a desire for order and predictability. The other side of the coin, which is hidden underneath, however, remains a discontinuous pattern of heterogeneous events that may not be so easily discerned. Science and religion have both been founded on the conviction that there exist hidden universal laws that can be uncovered; their difference lies in their methods of this expected discovery: through observation or belief. Neither has expected to account for a world of random events in which no rule can be observed or discovered. The tension between the events and regularity, however, remains. According to Ilya Prigogine, a Nobel laureate scientist, the law-event dualism forms a permanent tension in the history of Western thought.

Laws were associated to a continuous unfolding, to intelligibility, to deterministic predictions and ultimately to the very negation of time.

Events imply an element of arbitrariness as they involve discontinuities, probabilities and irreversible evolution. We have to face the fact that we live in a dual universe, whose description involves both laws and events, certitudes and probabilities. (quoted in Coveney and Highfield, 1991:16)

Measuring time through numbers and technological devices is one of a host of institutions that have been developed to manage change in society. Social institutions have been historically invented to regulate temporality and generate a sense of continuity and order. Spatial arrangements consolidate these approaches to temporality.

Locating time

An analysis of temporary events cannot be limited to their temporal dimension. Temporary events are not flashes in the void, but occurrences in particular locations, which is why an understanding of both space and time is needed in investigating temporary urbanism. Space and time are frequently mentioned within the same sentence, as they are seen as the two dimensions of reality or of our perceptions of the world. In the same way that conceptualizing time is intertwined with the construction of a social order, thinking about space has helped develop a systematic, single narrative about the multiplicity of objects, bodies and places.

Social space

The same basic questions about time are equally applied to space: does it exist as an independent entity or is it merely a set of relationships between objects and events? As we have already seen, these are ancient questions and have been a consistent theme in philosophy and science (Blackburn, 1996). The analysis of space has gone through three phases: common sense, abstraction and relativity (Cornford, 1976). Within the common sense perspective, which characterized most ancient civilizations, as well as in everyday life to this day, space is finite and relative, limited to the place that is occupied by bodies (Čapek, 1976; Gray, 1989). The abstract methods of thought in ancient Greece turned space into an abstract construct, associated with deductive thinking and philosophical thought (Faber, 1983; Algra, 1995). The Euclidean universe was a limitless void, and space was infinite without a centre or edge. This abstract space was 'an immeasurable blank field, on which the mind could describe all the perfect figures of geometry, but which had no inherent shape of its own' (Cornford, 1976:5). In the early modern age, Descartes and Newton embraced this concept to develop a new basis for the modern philosophy, mathematics and physics.

As an accomplished mathematician, Descartes revived the Euclidean concept of abstract space, devising the system of x/y coordinates to determine the location of points in space, a system that we are still using today (Smart, 1979:5). For Descartes (1968:56), space was 'a continuous body, or a space extended indefinitely in length, width and height or depth, divisible into various parts, which could have various figures and sizes and be moved or transposed in all sorts of ways'. Newton's physics was also based on the abstract concept of space, making up a universe subject to fixed mechanical rules. The early modern science until the nineteenth century was dominated by this notion of space, as a 'continuous, infinite, three-dimensional, homogeneous and isotropic' substance, without a preferred direction or difference between its points (Poincare, quoted in Torretti, 1984:25). Space was envisaged as 'an enormous stage, across which pass the events that make up the universe: the enduring stars, the brief particles, ourselves. Inside this box everything has its position, its path, and its time, and the business of the scientist is to give a rational account of it all' (Gray, 1989:176).

The existence of Euclidean space, however, was not easy to prove, posing a new ontological problem for science (Torretti, 1984:25). As with time, Leibniz refused the idea of space as an independent entity.

> I hold space to be something merely relative, as time is; that I hold it to be an order of coexistences, as time is an order of successions. For space denotes, in terms of possibility, an order of things which exist at the same time, considered as existing together, without enquiring into their manner of existing. And when many things are seen together, one perceives that order of things among themselves. (Leibniz, 1979:89)

This order, however, was interpreted in a number of different ways. For John Locke (1979:101–3), space and time were no more than distance and duration: space as 'the relation of distance between any two bodies or points'; and time as 'duration set out by measures'. This perspective sees space and time as measurable phenomena. Alternatively, how this order was perceived, according to Kant, was based on the observer, as time and space were not the dimensions of the world but of our own perception. Space and time, therefore, were only representations of appearances; they 'cannot exist in themselves, but only in us' (Kant, 1993:61). Space and time were not independent substances, but 'the necessary conditions of all our external and internal experience' and 'merely subjective conditions of all appearances, and not things in themselves' (Kant, 1993:64). Around the turn of the nineteenth century, the arrival of the non-Euclidean geometry and relative physics firmly established the relative concepts of space and time. Einstein's theory of relativity showed how space depended on mass and its motion, and how length and duration were relative to the motion of the observer (Jammer, 1954; Nerlich, 1994:267–8). Absolute or abstract concepts of space and time were ruled out as metaphysical, but the relative concepts were also thought to be no more than alternative interpretations rather than definite truths. As Albert Einstein wrote, the absolute and relative concepts of space are 'free creations of the human imagination, means devised for easier comprehension of our sense experiences' (Einstein, 1954:xiv).

Relative concepts of space and time were equally used by positive science to measure, account for and regulate the world. Relative space was the relationship between phenomena (Gregory et al., 2009), as exemplified by map-making, which is a representation of the patterns of concentration and dispersion of phenomena (Goodall, 1987). This representation, however, needs to be understood in the context of the social, political and economic conditions that produced that form (Massey, 2005). A relational concept of space, therefore, has attempted to locate it in the workings of society and its social relations. The idea of social space accounts for these social relations, and how space and its transformation are an integral part of the ways in which a society is organized (Lefebvre, 1991). Social space, as Bourdieu (2000, 134–5) puts it, is 'a structure of juxtaposition of social positions', which tends to be translated into physical space, so space becomes 'correspondence between a certain order of coexistence (or distribution) of agents and a certain order of coexistence (or distribution) of properties'. The notion of social space takes into account the role of the observer, the relationship between phenomena and the social context in which they are located. Like reified time, abstract space tends to fix spatial arrangements or provide a stable representation of spatial change. Temporary urbanism, however, may seem to be defying this stability, as it produces spatial flexibility through short-lived use of space as well as through the use of unpredictable and unfamiliar places. The concept of social space offers more flexibility in accounting for such fluidity, as it locates temporary events within a social milieu with all its dynamics of change. The question, however, is about the extent of flexibility or fixity of these social relations, which can solidify or liquidate the existing orders.

Controlled space

The idea of abstract space lay at the heart of the modernist architecture and planning; it emerged at the end of the nineteenth century, envisaging space as 'a positive entity within which the traditional categories of tectonic form and surface occurred' (Colquhoun, 1989:225). Geometry defined this space and technology shaped it. For Le Corbusier, 'plan' was the instrument to shape space, as it was understood through 'mass' and 'surface' (Le Corbusier, 1986:2–3). The earlier architectural tools for the management of time were attempts to slow down time and turn it into a predictable pattern. Cloisters, courtyards and enclosed squares were some of the examples of this management of time through spatial arrangement (Figure 2.6). The modernist architecture, in contrast, looked for speed and movement (Figure 3.9 in Chapter 3), hence changing its tools into functional ordering.

Functionalist architecture and planning defined the city according to its four functions of dwelling, recreation, working and transportation (Sert, 1944). Its attempt to reorganize space according to clear functions was associated with a functionalist concept of time, in which all the available time was divided into distinctive functions. While the details of working, dwelling and transportation were given explicit spaces of factory/office, home and roads/railways, the time and spaces of leisure seemed too amorphous, occupying the minds of many planners and architects in the mid-twentieth century. In such functional conceptualization, little time and space is left for spontaneous activities, where new things can happen without prior organization and planning. Activities that did not fit the clearly defined categories of work-rest patterns, which in turn

FIGURE 2.6 *Cloisters, courtyards and enclosed urban squares are a form of architecture to slow the flow of time and contain it within a predictable and manageable space (Brussels, Belgium).*

had been consolidated in land use patterns, would be a major challenge to the functionalist desire for order and clarity.

While time is all about change and movement, space seems to be about fixity and permanence, whereby things are defined by their dimensions and locations, given particular coordinates, relating phenomena to each other and to the places they inhabit and through which they are identified. The role of social institutions becomes the reproduction of these locational fixities. This is nowhere more explicit than in the laws and regulations that define property ownership. In this context, change and movement are a challenge to fixed arrangements, in the same sense that nomads have been a challenge to sedentary forms of life. Temporary events may be seen as incidences of nomadic experience, seeming to go against the fixities of space and social institutions, challenging the property laws, and undermining the planning rules.

Temporary events are allocated specific places, and many closed societies tend to limit the range of these events. Strong emphasis on traditions and social norms is the way that these unconventional events are kept at bay or ruled out. Public spaces of the city are often the places for such unpredicted and unpredictable events, places that are beyond the control of private owners, where things can happen without any particular impact on these fixed institutions. But not everything can be tamed through presence in the public, as Jane Jacobs (1961) had advocated for treating the strangers in the city. When faced with unregulated temporary events, however, the response by the legal and administrative frameworks has been reluctance and dismissal, as a wild card that cannot be tamed and therefore has to be limited or even eliminated. A prime example is the way the Roma population are treated by the local authorities and settled populations around Europe, whereby these mobile minorities have always difficulty finding a place for their temporary existence. Similarly, immigrants and refugees are treated as a disrupting force, which undermines the way space and time are regulated and the way social institutions and resources are used. To control unpredictability, functionalist design and planning has created specified places, such as children playgrounds, which replace the unregulated play of children in the streets in exchange for a safe place well supplied with playground furniture (Figure 2.7).

The temporary use of space is in many ways contrasted with the permanent control of space, a challenge to the more established forms of property ownership and use. Historically this form of use has been made possible through rent or other forms of permission to use space without undermining the owners' claim to the land and property in question. What characterizes the current trend in the temporary use of space is the much shorter timescale of this use. While traditional rent may be set for periods of months and years, the temporary use of space may revolve around days and weeks. When regulated,

FIGURE 2.7 *Playgrounds specialize space and allocate the function of play to specific areas, both protecting children from possible harm and confining them to predictable patterns of behaviour (Copenhagen, Denmark).*

it does not challenge the rights of the property owners, but it could unsettle the established views and expectations of the land and property markets.

As mentioned, property law and ownership is one of the primary institutions to control space and time. It recognizes someone's claim over objects and spaces, drawing permanent boundaries around land to prevent access by others, and therefore avoiding unforeseen changes. The control of property has been seen as a necessary foundation for society: 'The right of an owner of property to exclude all others from his property is one of the most prized – and most feared – rights any civilization can confer on its members' (Epstein, 1998:187). It is associated with projecting personal authority onto the material world as an expression of freedom (Hegel, 1967) and taming human aggression by giving it a physical target (Freud, 1985:303–4). It was, therefore, argued that 'property is the first embodiment of freedom and so is in itself a substantive end' (Hegel, 1967:42). This freedom is exerted within the private sphere, by limiting the influence of others within this realm.

Property ownership and law are closely intertwined. In fact the boundary that separated households from each other in ancient Greek cities was identified as the law (Arendt, 1958:63). When private ownership of property was challenged in the modern times as by Proudhon who called it theft, it was a call to arms against the established institutions, in which the systems of government and law are based on the protection of this boundary. Rousseau (1968:68) advocated that the individual property rights should 'always subordinate to the right of the community over everything'. More radically, Marx and Engels (1930:43) summed up their theory of communism in 'the pithy phrase: the abolition of private property'. While the boundary was an expression of permanence, predictability and continuity, questioning the legitimacy of the boundary was a challenge to an entire range of social institutions. These challenges, however, were not aimed at leaving the field in a permanent state of flux, but merely to change the existing arrangements with an alternative one, which would have its own forms of control, continuity, fixity, rigidity and desire for permanence.

Architecture is closely associated with property, as another social institution that offers a sense of permanence and continuity, with its origins in the transition from nomadic to settled life. After hunting, gathering and nomadic movement, the start of agrarian, sedentary life required the construction of a permanent settlement, embedded in the routines of agriculture and in the land that was being cultivated. Even before the identification of law with the boundary, the act of building permanent structures was an act of changing the temporality of social life, now locating itself in particular places on a permanent basis. The construction of a settlement was overcoming the temporary nature of nomadic life; architecture was the most visible and enduring sign of this desire for permanence. While hunters and gatherers may have economic and cultural linkages with a territory, farmers had to fix their territories further, as it was now necessary to work intensively on a piece of land, rather than merely collecting its natural produce. The nomadic tent was now replaced by the farmers' hut, which was a fixed point in the landscape. Fixing the territory, constructing a shelter and engaging with the land were all parts of establishing a new social order which was now expressed in the physical environment. Building, repairing and rebuilding structures would help establishing and reproducing a host of social institutions around this new social order (Figure 2.8).

Temporary urbanism, as a field of unprecedented and short-lived events is, therefore, considered a challenge to the fixed ideas and social arrangements. Temporary events are often limited to the public or semi-public sphere, where fewer exclusionary controls are in place. But there too the unprecedented events are regulated through the creation of routines and rhythms of urban life. These include the institutionalized repetition of events in the city, such as street markets and weekly events, which are regular in character, and mediating between the temporary and the permanent character of the city. The rhythms of life in the city, of children and adults going to and returning

FIGURE 2.8 *Nomadic life is always treated as a threat by the settled communities. A Roma camp on the edge of the city, next to the municipal waste disposal landfill site (Turin, Italy).*

from school and work, the opening and closing hours of shops, offices and factories are all part of the institutionalization of events through measured time. The social geography of the city and its physical landscape are shaped through these routines, supported by government laws and market incentives. As cities have grown larger and more complex, and manufacturing has been replaced by services, the patterns of urban life have become more diverse, as we will find out in the next chapter. The ability of the long-established social institutions to instil a sense of continuity becomes limited, as they come face-to-face with the impact of accelerated and instrumental temporality, revealing an inherent contradiction.

Conclusion

In various ways throughout history, time has been conceptualized as abstract, universal and linear, decontextualized from people and places, based on a mechanical model of universe, which is understood and governed by mathematical and technological methods. Technological change, from observing the projection of light on sundials to counting the beats of caesium in atomic clocks, has helped develop ever more precise ways of measuring time. A physical infrastructure has been developed to display time, turning an abstract concept into an empirical reality, an infrastructure of social life, which maintains the urban rhythms, showing how the universal and structured notions of time have framed the everyday life of the city. This conceptualization and quantification have been part of a process of creating social institutions that can manage change. A series of recurring institutions have been historically invented to generate a public infrastructure of meaning, a sense of continuity and order: property (claim over space, institutional recognition of time through property, drawing permanent boundaries around land), laws, institutions and traditions (reproduction of beliefs and practices), and cultural assets (from artworks to myths and legends). Spatial arrangements are the way social institutions, with their bid to conquer change and time, find material expression in stone, turning the invisible into the visible through their most permanent forms. Temporary events and structures, like the ways of nomads, are then considered to be a challenge to this fixed and sedentary pattern of life. They emerge as a series of fragmented occurrences in social space that appear to be decontextualized: out of place and out of order. But are they?

3

Accelerated Beats of Global Time

We have seen how time is conceptualized, measured and managed through mathematical calculations, social institutions and physical infrastructure, all attempting to frame and manage change, engendering a sense of stability and continuity. This chapter investigates how the city's rhythms are created and managed, and how technological and economic change has accelerated these rhythms, creating a sense of restlessness and ephemerality. In exploring the methods of mobility and organizing work, the chapter argues for the significance of technological and economic changes in how time is envisaged and managed in the city. Rather than confronting ephemerality, it seems that social institutions are inadvertently encouraging it. How can this be explained? The chapter argues that the processes of reification, quantification and commodification have paved the way for an instrumental treatment of temporality, turning it increasingly into the subject of market pressures for speed, productivity and profit maximization. The chapter starts by an analysis of innovation and its role in urban transformation. This is followed by five sections in which the social implications of technical and economic change are discussed: expanding time and space, filling the gaps, nomadic urbanity, radical simultaneity and illusions of immateriality, and disrupted institutions. This shows how adjustment to these changes and life through the accelerated beats of globalization have become an existential condition.

The analysis addresses the technical and economic changes that have transformed urban temporality and have provided a context for temporary urbanism. It investigates how the economic base of the city has been transformed, with dramatic consequences for urban life. Technological changes have gone hand in hand with historical change in the economic base of the city, from agriculture to trade, manufacturing and services. It engages with the making of cities. As the rhythms of global capitalism and the cycles of development get shorter, ephemerality is embedded in the cyclical nature of economic life, which creates periods of boom and bust, with considerable gaps in between. The linear and utilitarian attitude, which considers the city to be obsolete, demands adjusting the urban space to become 'fit for purpose', reflected in 'creative destruction', urban regeneration and renaissance, and gentrification of the city, as well as in inequality, informality and homelessness.

It also explores the impact of technological change on the city. Intensified movements of mobile populations, through tourism, migration and daily travel within urban destinations, generate a sense of transience in the city, as particularly reflected in central districts and urban gateways, in railway stations, ports and airports. Transience is also reflected in the speed of movement across the city, reducing contacts between people and places, reducing the urban experience to a detached gaze. Digital technologies and their impact on the sense of ephemerality are an integral part of this analysis. Cities of all kinds are connected, to varying degrees, through global networks, generating a new global sense of time, shaping and accelerating the rhythms of life in the city. These technologies have led to the idea of intangible products and virtual spaces, apparently undermining the materiality of the city. The chapter argues, however, that the so-called immaterial and aspatial economies are firmly rooted in material and spatial processes, and how the radical simultaneity of digital space has a history as well as a material and social context. Temporary urbanism is at once a reflection of and a driver for accelerated mobility and intensified connectivity, and the efforts to fill the gaps created by structural change.

Innovation and transformation

Innovation, broadly defined, is the generation of new ideas, methods, practices and products. There are extensive discussions of innovation in the fields of economic development and technological change, where innovation is thought to be the spearhead of economic change. The economic and technological aspects of innovation have been brought together by many analysts. The evolution of the human species has been associated with the technologies of fire, and the use of hand (Bradshaw, 1997). History has been periodized by technological innovations, such as in stone, bronze, and iron ages, considering the change from one technology to another to be an improvement for humankind's productive capacities. The organization of work and the distribution of power have been closely attached to this innovation.

For Karl Marx, the changes in productive forces were directly related to the changes in society. In a famous passage from 1847, he wrote:

> The social relations are intimately attached to productive forces. In acquiring new productive forces men change their mode of production, and in changing their mode of production, their manner of gaining a living, they change all their social relations. The windmill gives you society with the feudal lord; the steam-mill, society with the industrial capitalist. (Marx, 2008:119)

Extending this formula to our time would probably mean that computers will give you a global society and global corporations. More broadly, this change would entail many technological innovations in energy, transport and communications. Temporary urbanism, as a reflection of the accelerated speeds of a global society, would be directly aligned with this technological change, as discussed in this chapter. Technological determinism, however, is too reductive and unable to explain all the changes, as well as continuities, in social relations. It tends to concentrate on a single technology as the emblem of fundamental changes that may have occurred in society, producing a mythology around that technology and elevating it to the status of a defining feature of an age. But if we look at the history of the twentieth century, we see a number of such peaks, such as electricity, aviation, television, nuclear power, space travel, and container transport, each of which taken to signify a fundamental change, but soon giving way to the next innovation.

Instead of single technologies, Schumpeter (2003) emphasizes innovation as the driving force for change. Writing a century after Marx, his analysis of economic change is based on the internal dynamics of evolution, as in biological organisms, rather than outside forces such as revolutions and wars. This analysis involves temporal dynamics and is therefore a critique of the static understanding of economics with its emphasis on price mechanisms and fixed timeframes 'as if there were no past or future to it' (Schumpeter, 2003:84). In capitalism, he argued, the principal driving force in this evolutionary process is innovation, competition and the destruction of the obsolete remains of the past. Innovation, he wrote, is the 'fundamental impulse that sets and keeps the capitalist engine in motion', as manifest in 'the new consumers' goods, the new methods of production or transportation, the new markets, the new forms of industrial organization' (Schumpeter, 2003:83). It 'incessantly revolutionizes the economic structure *from within*, incessantly destroying the old one, incessantly creating a new one. This process of Creative Destruction is the essential fact about capitalism. It is what capitalism consists in and what every capitalist concern has got to live in' (Schumpeter, 2003:83).

The incessant transformation was based on long waves of technical and economic change, which had been formulated by Kondratieff (1935). History for Schumpeter combines linear and cyclical dimensions. A sequence of long-term cycles were each a distinct 'industrial revolution', starting from the 1780s and followed by others in the 1840s, 1890s and the 1940s, triggered by innovation in methods of production, commodities, forms of organization, sources of supply, trade routes and markets. Each cycle was marked by the emergence of a new productive apparatus leading to a period of affluence, even if punctured by shorter cycles of expansion and contraction, and ending with a period of decline and depression. At each cycle, it was imperative to eliminate the obsolete elements of the previous period, a creative destruction that initiated a 'process of recurrent rejuvenation of the productive apparatus' (Schumpeter, 2003:68).

The idea of creative destruction had already been formulated in the modernist architecture and planning. Le Corbusier's writings show the same attitude towards the remains of the past, which are considered to be obsolete and no longer functioning. The modernists thought that the European cities were obsolete, unable to accommodate the modern technologies of transport and therefore no longer fit for purpose. As Le Corbusier wrote in 1924, these cities' 'lack of order everywhere … offends us; their degradation wounds our self-esteem and humiliates our sense of dignity' (Le Corbusier, 1987:xxi). European cities needed wholesale transformation or were condemned to death, as 'They are not worthy of the age; they are no longer worthy of us' (Le Corbusier, 1987:xxi). Gradual renewal of the urban environment had always taken place, but now the productive forces of modern technology would facilitate wholesale change in ways that would not have been possible or imaginable to previous generations. While the idea of total transformation of the city may have taken a back seat in Western countries, it is a major force in the emerging countries like China, where a completely new urban landscape is rising.

The instrumental, techno-economic idea of innovation, however, has not disappeared from the Western agenda. It is present in the discussions about the knowledge economy and the role of innovation in economic development, especially in the context of a process of de-industrialization and the shift to services. In this context, creativity, design and innovation are defined in close relationship to one another. In a European Commission's attempt to measure these subjects, creativity and design were identified to spur innovation and have a positive impact on well-being and business performance (EC, 2009a:28). Creativity was defined as 'the generation of new ideas', design was 'the shaping (or transformation) of ideas into new products and processes', while innovation was 'the exploitation of ideas, i.e. the successful marketing of these new products and processes' (Hollanders and van Cruysen, 2009:5).

In a report commissioned by the UK government and headed by the chairman of the Design Council, Sir George Cox, innovation is primarily defined in a utilitarian way. As the Cox Review puts it, creativity is 'the generation of new ideas', innovation is 'the successful exploitation of new ideas' and design is 'what links creativity and innovation. It shapes ideas to become practical and attractive propositions for users or customers. Design may be described as creativity deployed to a specific end' (Cox, 2005:2). Rather than being identified as the process of generating new ideas, design becomes a translator of ideas into practice, art into utility.

These statements seem to portray creativity, design and innovation in a linear process, one leading to another. In practice, however, the creative path takes many different forms, and the processes of creation and application themselves inherently produce new ideas. In other words, new ideas are not created prior to a process of design and innovation, but are generated through these processes. Creativity unfolds in the activities of designing and implementing.

The statements also narrow down innovation to the conversion of ideas, products and processes into commodities. This is where an economic interpretation of innovation is used, whereby economic development is based on the creation of new marketable products and services. On this basis, when new products and services do not have an explicit commercial value, they may not be called innovative. Innovation, however, takes place in all aspects of life and cannot be limited to an economic framework and a utilitarian perspective.

Furthermore, discrepancies are held even within the marketable products and services as to what can be called creative and innovative. In urban and regional economics, a distinction is made between base activities, which are the goods and services that can be sold to people outside the region, and non-base activities are those that serve the local population's everyday needs (O'Sullivan, 2012). On the basis of this distinction, the base production is the source of income for a region and is therefore given priority over the non-base, which is thought to depend on the base for its expansion and contraction (Fujita et al., 1999:27). The problem with this distinction, however, is that it ignores the dependence of the base on the so-called non-base, as no activity flourishes in a void. This analysis generates a two-tier concept of society and of creativity, of the sort that is found in the idea of creative class, which privileges some sections of society as creative and relegates others to a mundane level (Florida, 2002). It fails to see the importance of the soil for the seed to grow, ignoring the significant innovations that take place in all aspects of society (Madanipour, 2011).

From an economic perspective, therefore, a short-lived event can become an innovative event if it generates goods and services that can be sold to people, in particular to those from outside the locality. The phenomenal growth of art exhibitions, cultural festivals and sports competitions, for example, can be analysed in this light, as they are temporary activities that can attract large numbers of outsiders to a locality, bringing in new sources of income. But even here, there is a two-way interaction between the event and the context. The existence of an infrastructure, a reputation, a history of an activity for an area may have important implications for the economic success or failure of an event. In other words, events do not take place in a void. They draw on an existing context which has been in the making for a long time. The short-lived event, therefore, would be performed in relation to this long-term context.

The idea of innovation, therefore, cannot be limited to converting ideas and practices into commodities. Generating new ideas and practices that could help people improve their lives, removing obstacles and overcoming limitations and exclusions, would also be innovative. It is in these activities that the creative potential of events can also be manifested. What are the innovative possibilities of temporary urbanism in all spheres of life, rather than in select parts, and for social and cultural benefits, rather than merely for economic ones?

Expanding space and time

Time and space are both mediated through technological change and organizational arrangements. Time and space, when reified, quantified and commodified, are understood as finite resources that offer opportunities but are also bound by limitations. When they are given monetary value and used as instruments in the calculative management of land, life and labour, a primary consideration becomes how to overcome their limitations and how to expand the extent and capacities of these finite resources as far as possible. Temporal and spatial expansion may, therefore, offer solutions to a mismatch between an activity and its time and space. Space is expanded through densification and relocation, while time is expanded through speed and multiplication. Temporary urbanism is closely related to these mismatches and the responding processes of expansion and adjustment (Figure 3.1).

If an activity grows in size, it requires more space, and so the limitations of space may be addressed by expanding an operation to its surrounding areas or relocating it to other places. Extending a house or redeveloping it into a newer, larger one is the on-site solution to spatial limitations. High-density cities, such as Tokyo, and many rapidly growing cities around the world, show how land is increasingly used more intensively, buildings are continually redeveloped, older ones being replaced by larger, taller structures, and narrower roads being replaced by wider, multi-level ones. Urban densities are increased as the balance between space and activity changes. Larger populations and higher

FIGURE 3.1 *Temporary use of space may be a pragmatic adjustment to the demand for space (Bellagio, Italy).*

rates of activities require more space, which is provided by densification and height. The distribution of higher densities, or the construction of tall buildings, may not be an accurate reflection of need and functionality, but of the workings of the construction and finance industries. With the expansion of consumerism, public spaces may be allocated to commercial operators, generating a source of income while animating the urban environment, both contributing to a functional and an aesthetic end (Figure 3.2). Nevertheless, spatial expansion does not take place in a void and it tends to reflect a growth in demand or supply. Similarly, urban shrinkage shows how space reflects the change in demand: as people move away from a declining city, its spaces become empty, either deteriorating or being demolished and cleared away.

In addition to on-site spatial adjustment, another spatial response to the mismatch between activity and space is relocation, moving to other places where the new spatial needs can be met. This is exemplified by moving to a larger (or smaller) dwelling, where the size and location of the dwelling offer new possibilities that were not available in the previous place. Examples include a larger (or smaller) office, which is better equipped and has easier access to transport infrastructure; a new factory that is nearer a pool of workers and better linked to its markets; the development of new towns and cities that can accommodate expanding populations; and even in the dream of space travel that can open up new possibilities for the future of humankind on other planets. They all are thought to open up new possibilities elsewhere, an option that is continually explored to overcome the limitations of space

FIGURE 3.2 *New street food stalls are introduced to animate the urban space and provide a source of income for the stallholders as well as the public and private operators (London, UK).*

here and look for it *there*. In rapidly growing cities, where economic vibrancy, immigration and natural population growth create high demands on space, vertical expansion and horizontal relocation are an integral part of the urban dynamics, as vehicles that help overcome spatial limits.

Similarly, the limitations of time reflect a mismatch between an activity and its available time, to which the responses have been speed and multiplication. As individual human beings, we are bound by the amount of time available to us: we can choose to be in another place, but not to be in another time; we can choose to enlarge our house, subject to the availability of means, but not to elongate our lifetime. Although medical advances have expanded the human lifetime, there are obvious limits to how far it can be extended. To do more in the time available, a solution has been speed, which has been a driving force in the development of new technologies. If we are able to reduce the time it takes to undertake an activity, we can do more of it within the time available. On this basis, technologies of transport and communication have been the most effective devices in temporal expansion. The technologies of movement, from taming horses to the invention of wheels, from building roads to making carriages and to the invention of aeroplanes have all reduced the amount of time it takes to move from one place to another. In parallel, the technologies of communication, from horse-driven couriers to the internet, have facilitated the transmission of information from one place to another in shorter periods of time. Speed of movement and communication, through the establishment of these technical networks, has fuelled temporal acceleration: to do more within the time available.

Expanding time may also be made possible through multiplication of human time, that is, through increasing the number of people who do the same activity. Working with an assistant would extend the time available to a craftsman. Mobilizing a team of volunteers or employing a paid workforce would extend the time that can be allocated to any activity. This is one of the main reasons for the emergence of cities, as it allowed the expansion of temporal resources by concentrating people in a relatively limited area, linking the capacities of different people to generate a larger pool of time. The development of reified and quantified concepts of time and of social institutions, as explored in Chapter 2, were instruments that helped manage this concentrated pool of time, locating time in particular places. In the Industrial Revolution, which started more than two centuries ago and is still unfolding in new parts of the world, the location of industries was closely associated with a large and expanding pool of labour. The energies of a single worker can only produce a limited amount of output, but the size of the new industries has needed massive amounts of human energy, which have been made accessible through the division of labour, as famously noted by Adam Smith (1993), and by amassing people in particular areas. Industrialization and urbanization have gone hand in hand since the nineteenth-century European industrialization.

In order to expand space and time, technological and organizational change has been essential. Technology is considered to be an abridged version of human work, facilitating the process of multiplication to an extent that could never have been imagined before (Smith, 1993). A machine would perform the task of a manual worker in a much shorter time, hence expanding the time available considerably. Manufacturing industries clustered manual workers but significantly magnified their productive capacities by the use of machines. A city as a concentration of workers and machines could expand time to unprecedented levels. A computer is capable of making calculations and data processing in sizes and speeds that could not be performed within the normal human capacity. While this seems to be dispersing the city and removing the need for concentration, by now we know that it has indeed had the opposite effect and cities are growing at a higher rate than ever before. In the same sense that transport technologies facilitated urban dispersion, but were ultimately the instruments of urban concentration, communication technologies enhanced new forms of connection, adding to the density of connections across space. What they offered was the possibility of interconnection between different places and activities. The process of concentrating and interconnecting productive powers, therefore, makes cities places of temporal densification and magnification, turning them into places of radical simultaneity, but always with spare capacities for undertaking new tasks.

Globalization is an organizational response to spatial and temporal limitations: extending time by relocation in space. However, globalization as a process of relocation is not merely an exercise in spatial and temporal expansion. Such an expansion might have been possible within regional and national territories, but it would have been subject to the regulations and frameworks which would have limited the expansion to some extent. Globalization is therefore a process of relocation that searches for expanding time and space while reducing costs and increasing profits. It is a process of relocating to places in which time may be magnified at considerably lower costs. By relocating the manufacturing industries to areas of the world that could offer a larger supply of time and space, in the form of labour and land, the industrialists could expand their operations. In this expansion, they look for advantages that would maximize the new spatial and temporal resources; therefore, they sought areas with lower costs of land and labour, weaker social and environmental regulations, and well connected to the transport networks, so that they could reduce the cost of production and their social obligations, while increasing their production and profit. While many companies initially announced their commitment to their original base, in which they had grown and succeeded, one by one they argued that they too needed to cut costs in order to survive in the global competition. However, it is often opening a space of possibility for the larger players, while closing down on the smaller, more vulnerable ones that could not compete.

Expanding time and space is the effort to facilitate access to these finite resources. This instrumental approach may be radicalized by resorting to a temporary approach to time and space. This contingent approach to time may open up the spaces of new possibility, but at the same time increases the sense of precariousness and insecurity. The context and rationale for this sense of contingency may be broadly summarized under the process of globalization.

Temporary use of space may be seen as a process of expanding space on a contingent basis, a process of creating a degree of flexibility in times of change. When an activity grows out of its space, its on-site expansion, spillover to the surrounding areas or relocation to new premises could take place on a cautious basis. Rather than buying or constructing new premises, renting provides a degree of exploration and flexibility which can be adjusted back if the new space is not really needed. Normal practices of renting, however, are based on contracts and agreements that may be too rigid for a variety of experimental or casual practices. This is why informal use of space, such as the occupation of parts of streets by street traders, is a temporary use of space on a highly precarious basis. Without access to property rights and permissions to trade, informal street traders live a precarious, temporary existence (Brown, 2006; Babere, 2013). Even more precariously is the case of relocation after disasters, when, after an earthquake or a flood, or after displacement through wars and conflicts, an entire tent-city may be erected for a short period of time as a response to the mismatch between people's need and availability of space.

The temporary use of space not only provides the possibility of spatial expansion through temporary access to new spaces. It also provides the possibility of multiple uses for the same space, a kind of inward and on-site expansion through multiplication. This is particularly the case with the events that unfold in public space. From street traders to weekly markets, from entertainers and protestors to large festivals and mass demonstrations, from moving across the city to lingering in street corners, public space provides the possibility of a flexible and multiple use of space. Multiple use of the same place for different purposes in different times of the day and night expands spatial affordance, offering new possibilities for a variety of activities within the same place, none of which is allowed to become permanent. Space can therefore be adjusted, expanded or contracted according to the different needs and demands, without resorting to a change of property ownership. Multiple use of space becomes a solution to the shortage of space for occasional and contingent activities. As public space is the most flexible space of a city, it is often, but not the only, the place in which this multiplicity is made possible.

Temporary urbanism is also a display of expanding time on a contingent basis. If time could be expanded through the multiplication of human labour, it could take a secure or contingent form. Long-term contracts or even lifetime employment was once the format with which many employers and employees thought about their relationship. Casualization of work, however, has transformed these relationships. Part-time, casual and non-contractual forms of work have provided the possibility of expanding time on a cautious, low-risk basis for the employers, without taking up a commitment to or an interest in the well-being of the employees. The pressure for labour market flexibility is a manifestation of this desire to expand time without expanding the level of commitment that may be associated with it. Labour market flexibility is also providing the possibility of speed as another way of expanding time. When the conditions of work can change at higher speed, it may provide the possibility of expanding or contracting time as and when needed, according to the conditions of the market. At the same time, it may make life highly precarious for the employees, who may find themselves permanently on the edge of a cliff, as any surge of the tide may turn their life upside down.

Filling the gaps: Mismatch between supply and demand

The cyclical nature of the market economy is reflected in the periods of expansion and contraction, which are accompanied by a parallel process of spatial production. The dynamics of capital drive the market economy, which 'represents an enormous productive potential but it is also a blind force' (Aglietta, 2000:397), regularly going through periods of crisis. The shorter economic cycles mark a crisis of overproduction, caused by a gap between the decline in demand and the continued supply of goods and services. The longer cycles are thought to be triggered by technological innovation, which transform the context of economic production, whereby some places and processes are considered obsolete and ready for 'creative destruction' (Perez, 1983; Schumpeter, 2003). The production of space and the operations of the land and property markets are an integral part of the market economy (Harvey, 1985; Lefebvre, 1991). Houses, shops, offices, roads and other spaces are produced or transformed in response to the signals of an expanding economy. At the same time the production of space finds a dynamic of its own, creating space as a way of feeding its own productive capacities, acting as a blind force in its search of perpetual expansion and higher rewards. The accelerated production of new space responds to, and feeds, economic expansion, but it inevitably comes to a halt with a period of economic slowdown and a crisis of overproduction.

The structural changes in society, meanwhile, continually transform the global division of labour (Madanipour, 2011). In response to the growing cost and complexity of working practices in the older industrial regions, investment in automation grew and manufacturing industries were relocated to low-cost regions, within a framework of deregulation and marketization. The de-industrialized regions embraced services as the basis of their economy, 'from metal-bashing to knowledge generation' (Stiglitz, 1999:15). Production and consumption, however, are always interdependent, and therefore the higher rates of global production needed higher rates of consumption. The implication for spatial production in de-industrialized contexts has been the growth of consumerist spaces, which have created shops, restaurants and leisure spaces for accommodating these growing sectors of the economy, while boosting the construction and finance industries with direct interest in spatial production. When the global crisis of 2007–8 hit, therefore, a mismatch between supply and demand in space emerged, which corresponded partly to the recurring cycle of expansion and contraction in the economy, and partly to the crisis of the overall model of consumerist, laissez-faire development which accompanied globalization (Barber, 2009).

The temporary use of space takes place in this context of a mismatch between supply and demand and a structural crisis of the economic development model. The recent global crisis and the longer term structural changes in urban societies have created spatial, temporal and institutional gaps, which are sometimes filled by temporary interventions, in search of interim solutions until the crisis is over. The immediate context of interim use is the global economic crisis, in which many activities were discontinued, businesses went bankrupt and spaces were empty or abandoned. It created mismatches between the supply and demand of space, which were addressed by finding interim use. The interim use is a mechanism for coping with crisis; it works in a short temporal cycle, and often it is not expected to provide any long-term solutions. As a result, the temporary use of urban space is widely talked about and practised these days, at times seen as a possible solution to some of the problems of urban development and management at a time of crisis.

According to the British Retail Consortium (2013), the trend of town centre shop vacancies in the United Kingdom continued to grow after the economic crisis of 2007–8, reaching 11.9 per cent. In the spring of 2013, according to the Local Data Company, the rate was higher: 14.1 per cent of the British shops were empty, compared to 3.3 per cent in September 2008 (LDC, 2013). At its peak in the summer of 2012, the rate of vacancy had reached 14.6 per cent, ranging from 10.7 per cent in London to 20.1 per cent in the northwest of England, reaching 30.6 per cent in a large city like Nottingham and 32.4 per cent in a medium-sized city like Dudley (BBC, 2012a,b,c). Although contested by the local authorities and town centre managers, these figures show the extent of vacancy in British high streets, which were hit by the global financial crisis and competition from supermarkets, suburban shopping centres and internet-based retailing. The smaller retailers cannot compete with four big supermarkets based on large sheds on the edge of cities, or with the phenomenal spread of online services, which is why the independent regulator for communication industries called the United Kingdom 'a nation of online shoppers' (Ofcom, 2013). Furthermore, the extent of shop closures reveals a crisis in the model of urban regeneration, which relied on creating spaces of consumption, and more broadly the problems of the consumption-based economy, which has been the driving force of the national economy for decades.

The result is a movement for finding alternative and interim uses for the empty shops. The UK government commissioned a report on the future of high street (Portas, 2011), and many have been engaged in reimagining the future of the high street (NEF, 2010). An Empty Shop Network was set up to offer information and advice on how to find and use empty spaces. Another network, London Pop-ups, lists the temporary restaurants, bars, galleries and gigs in the city, turning the idea of temporary use of retail space into a city-wide brand. It advises those who might be interested in setting up a temporary retail operation: 'A pop-up shop is a great hook to use to get press for your brand, so make sure you get the word out that you are offering something new and different for a limited time only' (Calladine, 2012). The idea is to turn the word 'pop-up' into a desirable brand. When established as such, even non-commercial activities may be presented under its banner to appeal to a young population (Figure 3.3).

The interim use may simply offer an opportunity to the users to benefit from low rents and the oversupply of empty spaces, as well as saving on the cost of construction and decoration in what is after all expected to run for a short period of time. Investors find the opportunity of expecting a return on their investment in a stagnant market, and public authorities the possibility of maintaining a degree of tax revenues and the appearance of vibrancy on the streets. Some see the temporary use of space as no more than an interim measure, filling a temporal gap until the good times return. According to the UK government, 'It is vital that we do all we can to enable vacant properties to be used for temporary purposes until demand for retail premises starts to improve' (DCLG, 2009:27).

Rent levels cannot be the sole consideration in a firm's decision to set up a temporary shop. As the *Vogue* magazine announced, Chanel opened its first

FIGURE 3.3 *Even non-commercial events are presented in the terminology and iconography of temporary urbanism to appeal to a young population (Newcastle, UK).*

stand-alone store in London as a pop-up shop in Covent Garden between July and December 2012 (Alexander, 2012). A major company like Chanel may not need the discounts on offer, but just to project a fashionable image, joining a trend. Claridges, one of the most exclusive hotels in London, set up a pop-up restaurant, in what seemed to be a desire to join a fashion trend. Some of the largest companies that have been engaged in the interim use of space, setting pop-up shops for brief periods, may not need the discounts on offer. Their usual style is to set up shop in the highest rent areas of a city, as their sense of their own prestige and market role would prevent them from going to low-rent areas. So the question is not the rent level on its own, but also the location of the space and the firm's position in a fashionable trend, although if high-rent locations can become available at a discount, they may be tempted. Furthermore, for some it is joining the fashion of the time, doing the cool thing, projecting a brand in a new light, which can stimulate their reputation in the marketplace and attract new clients. The downside, however, is that the entry of these giants to the temporary space market may deprive the smaller companies of their chances for using some of these spaces (Figure 3.4).

FIGURE 3.4 *Even large retailers feel the need to join the trend by creating temporary outlets (Milan, Italy).*

A neoclassical economic interpretation of the mismatch between supply and demand is based on the idea of market balance. If one side increases, the other side decreases to generate a balance. If the supply of a commodity rises, its price is lowered by the market so that the balance is restored. When a commodity is in short supply, however, the price rises to reflect this shortage. In the case of space and time, therefore, the oversupply of space and time leads to the slump in their price and the sometimes desperate attempts by the suppliers to find a solution. In this interpretation, temporary urbanism is a balancing mechanism, a response to the oversupply of space and time. As time and space cannot be easily reduced in quantity or be removed from the supply, in the form of labour force and built space, their unit price is lowered and alternative, interim uses are sought to fill the gaps. This interpretation, however, is a partial one, as the emergence of the mismatch is the result of many decisions made by powerful players in the political economy. What is termed as 'market correction', in which prices fall to reflect the crisis of overproduction, is endemic to the capitalist economy. Temporariness, therefore, is embedded in all aspects of economic production, where every human activity is commodified and the rules of supply and demand determine the status and value of a commodity in the marketplace.

The same phenomenon of the mismatch between supply and demand can be observed in offices, which have been created by the closure and downsizing of many companies, as well as by the overproduction of office space by speculative developers. At the heart of London's financial district, the rate of office vacancy grew by 50 per cent from 2007 to 2008 (Ruddick, 2008) and it reached 10 million square feet by 2009, that is, around 12 per cent of the City's office space (Ruddick, 2009). The mismatch can also be seen in housing, which has a much larger impact on the urban environment. The process of urban renaissance in the United Kingdom encouraged the development of residential units in town centres, which was primarily driven by speculative developments for higher-income customers. The economic crisis led to the collapse of housing market in British cities, particularly flats in city centres, some of which have remained empty for years (Punter, 2010).

The oversupply of residential space on a speculative basis is a worldwide phenomenon. In Ireland, a country with a population of 4.5 million, there were more than half a million dwellings built during the 1995–2005 decade. By 2012, 15 per cent of Irish homes were vacant. There were about 300,000 empty homes, with 1850 'ghost' housing estates unfinished (Flynn, 2012). In Spain, an estimated 1 million new homes were empty after the financial crisis and the collapse of the property market (Day, 2012). In the United States, the subprime mortgage crisis, which triggered the financial crisis, was caused by the oversupply of credit and space. Dubai, which seemed to be at one point a huge building site, was left with thousands of empty apartments (Spencer, 2010). In China, there were dozens of ghost towns built on a speculative basis, which were left vacant (Banerjee and Jackson, 2012), including the 'world's biggest mall' (Nylander, 2013).

In addition to speculative housing development, there is an oversupply of housing in shrinking cities, where the manufacturing industries have collapsed and the economic base of the urban area deteriorated. De-industrialization in the United Kingdom has left 1 million homes empty in British towns and cities, as people have left the cities for suburbs and other cities in search of work (Empty Homes, 2013). Industrial cities such as Liverpool and Manchester have lost much of their populations to industrial decline and suburbanization. Detroit has shrunk from a city of 1.8 million at its peak in 1950 to just around 700,000 population now (WSJ, 2011).

The market solution to the oversupply of residential units has been the price mechanism, dropping prices down to 50 per cent in a short period of time. In Ireland, residential property prices in 2012 were 64 per cent lower than 2007 (Flynn, 2012). In Spain, there was a 22 per cent drop in property prices between 2007 and 2012 and banks offered housing units at 50 per cent of their original prices to get them off their lists (Govan, 2012). In some cases, the property prices fell to a third of their original price (Brignall, 2012). The more radical solution, which requires government intervention, is demolition. In Ireland, the government acknowledged that the solution in some circumstances would be demolition (Kelly, 2011). In the United Kingdom, the controversial response to the oversupply of space in shrinking cities was demolition and redevelopment, as exemplified by Glasgow and Liverpool, which proved very unpopular.

Abandonment, loss of value and demolition, however, do not offer temporary use for space. As the case from empty shops, offices and homes shows, the interim use may be applied to spaces that have clear designations and are owned and controlled by a person or an organization. Permanence is expressed in the principle of property ownership, which is institutionalized by law and documented publicly. While properties may change hand through exchange, fixed property boundaries and legal frameworks that support them maintain a sense of continuity and permanence. The interim use of space does not undermine this historical arrangement, but merely helps it overcome its short-term crises. The existence of this control would allow the use of space as filling a temporal gap, waiting for the market to pick up again, the demand to rise and the property regain its pre-crisis value.

Another scenario in the mismatch between places and activities is when demand is higher than supply, when there are too many activities and too few places that can accommodate them. This is evident in the problem of housing. In the United Kingdom, a crisis of housing has gripped the country, resulting from a spatial mismatch of supply and demand, where the supply of affordable housing in areas in need has not been met, and where the gentrification of urban areas has priced out low-income households, while the overproduction of upmarket housing and the decline of population in shrinking cities have led to an oversupply of space. The government efforts to sort out this problem has been putting pressure on the planning system to be more flexible, removing the obstacles to house building and conversion of some of the office space oversupply to housing, each open to debate and controversy. In growing cities such as London, however, the demand has remained high, where international investors compete for space with local communities, leading to a housing crisis in which many lower income and young people cannot afford to have access to decent and affordable housing.

The size of the problem and the structure of the market make the temporary use of space far more difficult in the case of housing. Squatting, which is a form of temporary use of space to address an acute problem, meanwhile, is resisted. For example, some who had lost their homes in Spain's economic crisis attempted to squat in empty buildings, explaining their action only as avoiding homelessness (Day, 2012). The number of squatting cases in many large cities around Europe is considerable, either as a form of protest (e.g., Naples) or simply a solution to homelessness (e.g., Manchester). However, this form of temporary use of residential space is limited in size and challenges the legal frameworks of property ownership. It is not accidental that it was made illegal in the United Kingdom in 2012 (Figure 3.5).

FIGURE 3.5 *The ultimate expression of precarity is homelessness, which is widespread even in rich cities (Paris, France).*

In the case of undersupply of space, the interim use of space offers the possibility of coping with crisis and overcoming the mismatch between space and activity. This mismatch may be due to the users' difficulties or places' limitations and problems. Street traders in many parts of the world are users who do not have access to permanent spaces for trading, which is primarily a question of access to resources (Figure 3.6). Temporary and precarious use of space is a way of coping with the crisis of poverty. The difficulty in space is exemplified by disaster-struck areas, where wars and natural disasters have demolished or removed access to urban areas. In response, temporary cities are created, with tents or containers, which offer relief for what is hoped to be a brief period before reconstruction can start and a return to normal urban life can be possible.

The problem of mismatch between supply and demand for space can be compared to the problem of labour's supply and demand and the informal economy. De-industrialization created large-scale unemployment in some areas, creating a surplus of labour force that needed to be redeployed. One answer has been the rise of casual, part-time and precarious employment, which is a temporal solution for an economic problem. Both are examples of the contingent use of resources in uncertain circumstances. What is known as zero-hour contracts now shapes the primary working conditions of hundreds

FIGURE 3.6 *Without access to secure employment or place of trade, street trading is the economic manifestation of temporary living for millions of urban inhabitants (Medellin, Colombia).*

of thousands of workers, whereby they do not know how many hours a week they may be able to have a paid job, as their employers are not willing to make any commitments. Although the frameworks and dynamics of labour market are different from land and property market, they are both subject to the same macro-economic circumstances and the same logic of the market, where work and space are treated as commodities that are exchanged in the marketplace. Casual use of labour and temporary use of space, therefore, may have parallels in their economic dimension.

A temporary state may therefore offer a pragmatic use of in-between spaces, filling the spatial and temporal gaps, offering interim and multiple uses of space, as a way of coping with crisis, responding to a mismatch between the supply of and demand for space. These gaps and interventions, however, are ambivalent in nature, as they can be used as vehicles for moving simultaneously in different political, economic and cultural directions. Depending on who is involved and to what purpose, the interventions may have completely different characters and outcomes. Rather than merely responding to a crisis, it may show an opportunistic attitude, trying to take advantage of uncertain situations, resulting in extra layers of precariousness for vulnerable populations.

Nomadic urbanity

Expanding space and time and concentrating them in cities rely on interconnectivity across the urban space, on speed and intensification of movement, which lead to heightened mobility and a perpetual sense of temporary experience, especially in larger cities. Intensified movements of mobile populations, through daily travel within urban destinations, tourism, business and large-scale migration, generate a sense of transience in the city, as particularly reflected in central districts and urban gateways, in railway stations, ports and airports, in business and leisure districts. Transience is also reflected in the speed of movement across the city, minimizing contacts between people and places, reducing the urban experience to a detached gaze. While it might have horrified nineteenth-century observers such as Engels, by now such disconnection has become commonplace, a desired state, a refuge from the social intrusions and absence of freedom in parochial places. In villages and small towns, the social fabric offers support but also demands conformity, applying a degree of social surveillance that would be at odds with the freedoms that many may seek. The trade-off between social support and freedom is a major challenge for modern societies, where the big city offers freedoms that the small town would deny.

From the invention of trains to the large-scale travel by planes, the technologies of transport have created the possibility of speeding across space, generating the idea of being free from the constraints of the localities (Figure 3.7). A first-time train passenger wrote in 1830, 'We flew on the wings of the wind at the varied speed of fifteen to twenty-five miles an hour, annihilating "time and space"' (quoted in Gleick, 2000:52). The possibility of speed and connectivity created this feeling of overcoming the obstacles that time and space had imposed on human experience, which was now celebrated as their concentration and even disappearance (Johnston et al., 2000). Therefore, the impact of speed on time and space has been interpreted as their annihilation, convergence (Janelle, 1968), and compression (Harvey, 1989), stretching social systems (Giddens, 1984) and producing 'timeless time' (Castells, 1996). Transport networks link people and places across the globe, giving the impression that the world has been shrunk to the size of a village (Figure 3.8). Time and space, as existential limitations, were now thought to be defeated through new ways of mobility and contact. The social institutions that were created to safeguard space and time would be also defeated and transformed. The meaning and value of place has been replaced by 'the strategic value of the non-place of speed' (Virilio, 1986:133).

FIGURE 3.7 *The continuously mobile urban population creates the conditions of nomadic urbanity (Tokyo, Japan).*

FIGURE 3.8 *Transport hubs are the focal points of multiple rhythms and speeds, the meeting points of the nomadic urban populations, and the catalysts of future urban development (Vienna, Austria).*

At the same time, this freedom from the context would create a new nomadic experience, as what kept people rooted in particular places was now being unsettled, allowing large numbers of people to be uprooted from their places and be thrown into the maelstrom of modernity. In the nineteenth century, trains offered a degree of freedom, allowing people to leave their towns and villages and see the world outside. The sense of permanence which was associated with ever-repeating rhythms of life in agrarian settlements was now disrupted by the possibility of movement, generated by the demands of the new industries that were hungry for raw materials and workforce. Trains facilitated the concentration of people and workplaces in large cities, nodes to and from which raw materials and manufactured goods could be transported (Briggs, 1968). When the technology of trains was employed for urban journeys, it allowed the suburbs to develop, the city to grow in all directions and travel across the city to become faster and easier. The invention of elevators facilitated the upward growth of cities, the start of building higher and higher towers, densifying parts of cities. Accelerated movement in horizontal and vertical directions was now made possible, speeding up the rhythms of life while subjecting them to new patterns of work and rest.

With the arrival of cars, movement across space was made more flexible in many ways: a car could take a small number of people in almost any direction; these journeys, however, would rely on access to a car and the existence of roads. To provide for these requirements, methods of mass production, such as those pioneered by Ford, were used to produce cars in large numbers. The programmes of road building from the early twentieth century started to open up the spaces of the city to cars. The spaces of existing cities were adjusted to the cars, while new spaces were built on the basis of car access. As the most versatile forms of movement, cars became the determining feature of modern urban life, mobilizing all the resources to reorganize the urban space around the freedoms that cars offered. The modernist architecture and town planning emerged as the technical and cultural instruments that would advocate and facilitate this adjustment.

The modernist recipe for a functional reorganization of the city, not only to accommodate the car but also to give it primacy over other considerations, was widely adopted and implemented throughout the world (Figure 3.9). As Le Corbusier (1987:179) wrote, in the 'age of motor-cars', 'the city made for speed is made for success'. Seeing cars in motion had overwhelmed him, filled with 'an enthusiastic rapture', which was 'The simple and ingenuous pleasure of being in the centre of so much power, so much speed' (Le Corbusier, 1987:3–4). This, he thought, was the dawn of a new society, and a new city was emerging that would condemn the old city to destruction and disappearance paving the way for this new world. Movement, therefore, became the motto of the modernist thinking, not only in the possibility of moving from one place to another at high speed, but also movement in single

FIGURE 3.9 *Facilitating the speed and volume of movement is a defining feature of city building (Tokyo, Japan).*

places. The futurist painters depicted their subject at all stages of movement, while cubist artists showed their subject from a variety of angles, moving around to register its different faces (Giedion, 1967). Meanwhile, the new art of cinema offered the possibility of capturing and showing movement.

Trains, underground railways, cars and buses are all used on a network of roads and railways that are densified in converging nodes such as railway stations and car parks. Together, these spatial fragments make an interconnected infrastructure for movement. Together with the systems of time measurement and display, which we discussed in Chapter 2, they constitute a public infrastructure of time in the city. They keep time and ensure that the life beats of the city are maintained and accelerated. These beats were in line with the functional patterns of work in an industrial society: the daily beats of work and rest, commuting between home and work, suburbs and city centre. The spatial structure of the city was, therefore, shaped in accordance with this public infrastructure of time and the social organization of work. Functionalist planning was the spatial instrument that ensured the translation of the social organization of working and living into the spatial infrastructure of the city. As T.S. Eliot wrote in his *Choruses from the Rock*, London was a timekept city: the way people worked and rested, how they moved between the city and suburbs, and how they lived their lives were all ruled by time (quoted in Elton and Messel, 1978:102).

This accelerated system was constructed on the basis of the routines of industrial work, but, with the transition from manufacturing industries to services as the basis of the urban economy, these routines were broken and became much more diverse and fluid. The patterns of work and rest may still be dominated by the morning and evening travel to and from work, but it has become far more differentiated than before. The industrial order was dismantled with de-industrialization and globalization, the widespread use of information and communication technologies, the privatization of public transport and many other public institutions, and increased migration to larger cities. Hyper-diversity and hyper-mobility of the population in large metropolitan areas have set the scene for the new urban century. While the smaller towns and cities may appear to have kept their slower paces and less diverse populations, their conditions of life have also changed dramatically, as globalization connects places to each other and makes them interdependent. The public infrastructure of time that had been created for the industrial city, with the social institutions that supported it, had to be dismantled or transformed to allow for the emergence of a new one. The challenge was now creating a new social order while giving birth to a far more fluid society.

A new concept and a new public infrastructure were needed for time. The order of events, which constitutes the heat of this temporal infrastructure, had to be reshaped. The conditions of reification, quantification and commodification of this order have provided the basic stability of a system which is being subject to the continual turmoil of heightened competition. Temporary urbanism is one of the ingredients of this new arrangement, both as a sign of change and as a driver for change. In the world of work, temporary contracts and working arrangements have become commonplace, creating a sense of permanent insecurity in the working population. In the world of everyday life, the experience of hypermobility gives rise to a sense of being continually on the move, with limited contact with places and people, generating the feeling of being a short-term visitor at all times, a permanent tourist. In social encounters, the hyper-diversity of populations generates a sense of detachment from the unfamiliar others and accentuates introversion for floating and detached individuals. The urban experience, especially in large urban areas, becomes a nomadic experience. While this nomadism may free people further from the familiar contexts, it also undermines the social institutions and the age-old attempts at managing the human feeling of vulnerability to change. Measuring and accounting for time was a way of coming to terms with change. Now change has become so prevalent and at such high rates that temporariness becomes the norm rather than the exception. Competition, which is the primary purpose of neoliberalism (Foucault, 2008),

FIGURE 3.10 *International events, such as the Expo, are used to enhance the global reputation and competitiveness of cities, turning the city into a stage, and linking the temporary to the permanent (Milan, Italy).*

creates a sense of continuous uncertainty, a situation of permanent risk, rendering all experiences potentially a temporary one. Competition as the driving force of social change becomes the primary institution around which temporality is reshaped (Figure 3.10).

Radical simultaneity and the illusions of immateriality

In addition to heightened mobility and diversity, the technologies of information and communication have accentuated the experience of nomadic urbanity through radical simultaneity and illusions of immateriality. Instant connections across the world give the impression of radical simultaneity, whereby time seems to have become an intensified present-time for those connected to these networks. Digital products, meanwhile, have created the impression that economic production is now intangible and immaterial. Both of these illusions of simultaneity and immateriality, which are the outcomes of digital technologies, intensify the sense of ephemerality and temporariness.

Digital technologies have penetrated deeply into the lives of many people around the world, to the extent that it is thought that we are living in a digital age (Avery et al., 2007), a computer age (McLuhan, 1964), an internet age (Nicholas, 2000; Cavanagh, 2007; Raymer, 2009) and an information society (EC, 2009b; ITU, 2009). Using particular technologies to define an age is not new: history has been divided into stone, bronze and iron ages; more recent periods have been called industrial, atomic and space ages. Those who believe in long techno-economic waves think that a major technology brings along a wave of innovation and determines the primary driver for social and economic change (Kondratieff, 1935; Perez, 1983).

The shaping of cities and the cultures of design were associated with the dominant technical device of the time: mechanical clocks inspired city design in the Renaissance and Baroque periods; manufactured machines inspired the nineteenth and twentieth century; and computers and communication networks the latter part of the twentieth century onwards (Madanipour, 2007; 2011). The world was envisaged as a clock, a machine or a network, and each time the city was to be designed on that basis. The quasi-animated and magical universe of the Middle Ages was first replaced by a mechanical conception of the world, in which world was likened to a clock, with a visible face and hidden orders of wheels and springs that could be discovered by science (Whitrow, 1972; Hollis, 2002). City design took on a mathematical outlook expressed in the geometrical regularity of a system of nodes, axes and networks that were superimposed on what was considered to be disorderly medieval cities. Manufacturing industries inspired the next phase of designers who wanted to rebuild the city in the image of a machine, looking for a new visual and spatial language that was inspired by engineering and manufacturing industry (Le Corbusier, 1986). Trains and cars, as well as computers and communication networks, were the paradigmatic source of inspiration for reshaping the cities in the image of networks: both shaped as a network of transportation and communication and as nodes in global networks (Figure 3.11).

Dominant technology is also associated with the dominant form of power: As Marx famously wrote, 'The windmill gives you society with the feudal lord; the steam-mill, society with the industrial capitalist' (Marx, 2008:119). Following this logic, the computer would now give you the global corporation. Such forms of naming and association, however, can be reductive. It would be problematic, both empirically and normatively, to think of a single form of society dominated by a single technology. It would be 'extremely misleading to talk of "*the* information society"' (Gershuny, 1983:232), and it would be 'inadmissible' to envisage the outcome of technological change to be leading to 'a narrow, fatalistic technological determinism – to a single possible form of society' (UNESCO, 2005:17). In short, a single technology may carry the flag of identity for any particular period of time, but it always exists alongside

FIGURE 3.11 *Global communication networks link the four corners of the world together, generating radical simultaneity, even in unexpected places (Istanbul, Turkey).*

many other forms of technology and social relations; both those that have existed in the past and are deeply embedded in social relations, and those that are nascent in current circumstances and will emerge one day to shape new directions.

Digital technologies are closely linked to an altered sense of temporality: the sense of immediacy and simultaneity, and the pressures for acceleration, that are brought about by the reach and speed of these technologies. If people from across the world can be in touch with a multitude of others at the same time, and if information, goods and services can be transmitted in an instant, the sense of annihilating time and space is intensified. This intensified temporality plays a key role in accelerating the pace of urban life, generating the impression of a twenty-four-hour world, which never goes to sleep, and which is driven by a cacophony of never-ending global beats. This feeling is heightened in the centres of global networks, such as in London and New York, but also felt throughout the world, albeit in different forms and levels of intensity. Temporariness is a direct outcome of this acceleration, as global connectivity continually brings about new ideas and practices, and increases pressures on localities to conform. As Michel Foucault (2008) argued, the primary feature of neoliberalism is inducing the sense of competition in society. When this competition is globalized, almost everything in every place becomes the subject of competition with a multitude of others across the world, continually throwing everything into the air.

One of the ideas that has been used to describe the digitally mediated globalized economy is to call it a knowledge economy which is weightless and immaterial (Madanipour, 2011). The knowledge-based economies are defined as being 'directly based on the production, distribution and use of knowledge and information' (OECD, 1996:8), reflecting the change from producing steel and cars a hundred years ago to knowledge and information today (Stiglitz, 1999:15). This transition from accumulation of physical capital to knowledge (UNESCO, 2005:46) and the intangible nature of its products have given the impression that this is an immaterial, intangible or weightless economy (Quah, 2002). After all, the computer programs and games are only digital streams, forms of expression made through electromagnetic processes and communicated through invisible networks. The products of this economy are thought to be immaterial and aspatial, as they are 'not localized to a physical spatial neighbourhood' (Quah, 2002:383). Consequently, many aspects of life are also called immaterial: labour (Lazzarato, 1996; Hardt and Negri, 2000), culture (Thomas, 2008), society (Diani, 1992), architecture (Hill, 2006), etc. In the visual culture where image rules (Debord, 1994) and symbolic production is contrasted with the material culture, cyberspace is thought to be an independent realm detached from the norms and conditions of the material world (Nayar, 2010). This concept of immateriality and aspatiality fuels a sense of ephemerality and detachment.

Announcing the death of the material world, however, is premature. If the electromagnetic processes and wireless networks cannot be seen or touched, it does not mean that they are not material. The atomic and subatomic worlds are indeed the foundations of the material reality, rather than an alternative realm. The idea of immaterial economy may refer to the intangible nature of its products, which are not as bulky as the manufactured objects such as cars and refrigerators, and that they are easy to transmit across the world in an instant. However, this lightness is transformed into heaviness in a number of ways. The production, distribution and consumption processes of these products are as material as any other economy. They rely on people who live everyday lives, with homes, shops, schools and hospitals. Meanwhile, the amount of material objects that the citizens of rich nations consume would probably be far more than ever before, as the production of consumer items and the disposal of their waste have been relocated to other parts of the world. They all take place within particular times and places, rather than in a timeless time and placeless place. The idea of intangible products and immaterial economy would therefore be a metaphor rather than a description of reality.

Disrupted institutions

In addition to the technologies of making, the technologies of organizing have been instrumental in temporal expansion. The new division of labour has been recognized as the principal reason for higher productivity. Spatial and temporal expansion, however, cannot leave these cultural instruments intact, as the dynamism and vibrancy of the modern city unsettle and dislocate the temporal and spatial orders. Globalization accentuates this disruption further.

Conceptualizing time as a resource and trying to expand it lead to tensions with the social institutions that have been at work to manage and regulate temporality; while these institutions reflect a need for stability and continuity, temporal expansion challenges and destabilizes these institutions. The result is an acceleration of temporality and the instability of social institutions that are under pressure to adapt to rapidly changing circumstances.

Within single territories, spatial and temporal expansions are subject to a series of restrictions, which are increasingly relaxed as a result of globalization. Temporal practices have long been subject to laws and regulations such as the limitations on opening hours of shops and offices. The routines and the working hours of schools, factories and offices have shaped the life beats of the industrial city. The morning and evening rush hours, the commute to work and school, and the weekly shopping routine have all been an essential part of the modern temporality. With globalization, and the predominance of services as the primary pattern of work, however, these routines have become diversified, generating a far more complex pattern of temporality in which the hours and places of work and rest are more flexible.

Spatial changes are also subject to laws and regulations, as best exemplified by city planning, which frames the possibility of vertical and horizontal expansion of the city, protecting some spaces as historic or green areas, and designating other areas for growth (Figure 3.12). The London Plan, in which these areas of development opportunity are earmarked, shows the possibilities and limits of spatial expansion in a vibrant, growing city. Spatial solutions are also subject to the availability of resources and price mechanisms of the market. The property markets largely determine the shape of the spatial expansion, so those activities that promise a higher return on property investment are given priority. In housing and the range of other activities, therefore, the prosperous parts of the town are given priority by the market operators over the lower income areas. Moreover, spatial expansion may become a primary economic activity, so there may be new developments that are driven by the mechanics of the property market, rather than being a response to the social needs. When property ownership and exchange becomes a driver of the economy, spatial expansion is based more on pure economic calculations, rather than a solution to spatial limitations.

FIGURE 3.12 *The reintroduction of a stream has opened up the space of possibility for leisure and temporary events, as well as changing the property market in the area (Seoul, Korea).*

Globalization is a deepening of instrumental modernity, which first arose in the eighteenth and nineteenth centuries in Europe. It expects all the social institutions and spatiotemporal arrangements to be revisited in the light of new ideas and practices. On this basis, the ideas of temporality that had been developed in previous periods were all opened up to critical scrutiny and subsequent revision or replacement. Competition determines a framework and an atmosphere in which nothing can stand still, as it is thought to be leading to stagnation and decline. The instrumental attitude of capitalism and the critical attitude of modernity, however, are not limited to the ideas and practices of the past, but also to the new ones as they emerge and as soon as they are considered to be obsolete, incapable of coping with the ever-changing circumstances that modernity would bring about. Every idea and practice at any moment would be open for revision and adjustment. With globalization, this critical fluidity and flexibility has been extended to the globe, a process that had already started with colonialism, now intensifying through new technologies and the willing participation of the local elites.

In this context, the long process of reification and institutionalization of time has come under continuous pressure to adjust and change. Social institutions become much more fluid, so as to cope with these rapidly changing circumstances. Short-lived events and temporary urbanism reflect this sense of fluidity. Temporariness, meanwhile, is turned into a new institution itself, constantly unsettling the established institutions, a permanent cultural revolution. It becomes a form of counter-institutionalization, in which the existing arrangements are not taken for granted anymore and processes of experimentation, as well as symptoms of insecurity and vulnerability, are displayed. Permanent change means all ideas and practices are taken as interim, everything being open to transformation at a moment's notice, which is a hallmark of modernity.

Modernity, and its extension through globalization, therefore, dislocates time. Time, as we saw, has been a measure of change, located in places and social institutions. Globalization spreads time and disconnects it from any particular location. Now there is almost no location that is disconnected from this global time, which is characterized by continuous and faster paces of change. Change, rather than continuity, is the primary feature of an interconnected global space-time. Political and cultural revolutions were staged to accelerate this process of change, but not knowing that their outcome may not become a new, settled arrangement. A primary example is Mao's cultural revolution in China, which was meant to destabilize the established routines of the society by turning everything upside down, with disastrous results for its victims. The unforeseen results also included the destabilization of the destablizers, paving the way for the emergence of a completely new spatiotemporal order. In the 1960s, Mao initiated a cultural revolution in communist China so as to turn everything upside down in his country, creating the conditions of temporariness which in fact paved the way for opening the society to market forces within a decade. Temporariness shakes up the settled ways only to change them in fundamental ways.

An existential condition

A temporary state may even become an existential state, living always in in-between spaces, a permanent destination in itself, a way of being. It can be the result of the repetition of temporary events, or more broadly, an underlying condition, a reflection of the speed of change and the precariousness and transience of life in modern urban societies.

The temporary use of space is not new. The temporary use of space is the opposite of the permanence inherent in fixed objects and land and property ownership; but even the permanence of ownership appears to be temporary when seen within longer historical or environmental perspectives, whereby entire cities can emerge and disappear within a relatively short period of time. Historically, overcoming the sense of transience and managing change have been made possible through the generation of fixities such as monuments, social institutions and routines. Monuments have been used to create fixity and defy ephemerality since the ancient times, while other fixities have been created through the repetition of temporary events, such as the weekly and seasonal markets, or the temporary extension of activities from one place to another.

Cities, as they emerged in the nineteenth century, were places of manufacturing industries and mass customs of the blue-collar workers, going through standardized routines of life, leisure and labour. The modernist architecture and planning attempted to give shape to this mass society with the help of modern technology, by the mass production of buildings and the functionalist organization of urban space. Speed and movement were the essential ingredients of modernist design and development (Giedion, 1967; Le Corbusier, 1987). It was part of a larger movement in the past two centuries that attempted to create an organized society out of the influx of uprooted people who congregated in cities. With intensified globalization, however, manufacturing industries are relocated to new areas, replaced by services and a consumption-based economy. Mass routines give their place to more flexible ways of living and working, and the idea of functionalist and comprehensive organization of the entire urban space is abandoned in favour of localized transformations, strategic and selective planning, and project-based changes. As markets demand increasing flexibility, and as technologies accelerate the pace of change, temporary urbanism becomes ingrained in all aspects of urban life. The underlying condition of the modern urban life, therefore, becomes a constant state of flux, in which events unfold at high speed. With this hypermobility comes transience, diversity, alienation, multiple and disjointed identities, inequality, vulnerability and precariousness, protest, and uncertainty.

The urban space is the stage on which it all unfolds. Street traders in many parts of the world are those who do not have access to permanent spaces for trading, which is primarily a question of access to resources. Temporary and precarious use of space is a way of coping with the crisis of poverty. The difficulty in space is exemplified by disaster-struck areas, where wars and natural disasters have demolished or removed access to urban areas. In response, temporary cities are created, with tents or containers, which offer relief for what is hoped to be a brief period before reconstruction can start and a return to normal urban life can be possible.

Conclusion

Economic and technological changes have accelerated the beats of social life: the globalization of industrial production and the shift from manufacturing to services, alongside the development of information, communication and transportation technologies, all speeding up the rhythms of life and unsettling the traditional institutions and efforts at managing change. They represent the challenges of a new techno-economic order to an older one, bidding to replace it by disturbing its temporal certainties. In this new order, tangible products are replaced by intangible ones, factories by flexible offices, mass routines by diversified patterns of work and life, all demanding and shaping new forms of temporality. Temporary urbanism seems to be in line with these changes, reflecting and mediating the transition from one order to another. The dynamics of expanding time and space show how the mismatches between activities and their space/time are addressed through densification, relocation, acceleration and multiplication, all features that are amply manifested in globalization. Temporary interventions reflect the patterns of expansion and contraction of time and space, whereby the gaps that are created as a result of globalization are filled by temporary activities. The technologies of transport, information and communication have intensified the speed of movement and connectivity, generating the illusions of aspatiality, immateriality and ephemerality, and challenging the concepts of temporality and the social institutions that were created to stabilize and manage change.

PART TWO

Existential Temporality

The two chapters in this part show the intuitive sense of temporality as an existential condition, and how the processes of instrumentalization and acceleration of time have had an impact on this temporality, generating anxiety and disconnection.

4

Temporality, Memory and Identity

In the previous two chapters, I explored the way time is conceived as a substance, and measured and turned into a commodity, with all the associated social institutions and material environments. This essentialized and commodified concept of time was expanded to many new parts of the world to construct a universal temporal framework, and an accelerated pace of time that could maximize its instrumental use. I also explored a second concept of time as the order of events, which in a somewhat similar way has been employed to regulate social behaviour and impose a coherent order on the various events and processes. In this chapter, I will explore another perspective into time: the personal sense of time and its complex relationship with instrumental notions of time. The chapter shows how this phenomenological temporality and the processes of memory and identity are disrupted by such acceleration. Meanwhile, phenomenological continuity itself is open to questioning, as the inner time is multiple and fragmented, with different responses to chronocratic acceleration.

The chapter examines the existential unfolding of time at the intersection of phenomenological time, memory and identity. The main argument is that subjectivity, memory and identity are the key features of existential temporality, and that their disruption or loss leads to cultural amnesia, a sense of transience, loss of collective memory, and fluidity and multiplicity in the common frameworks of meaning and identity, while a sense of continuity and a hope for psychological security may persist in many traces. At the same time, the intuitive temporality itself is not a continuous fabric, as it is subject to the fragmentation of selves and events. The chapter is, therefore, organized in four parts: inner phenomenological time, memory and the reconstructed time, identity and the narrated time, and the multiplicity of the voices and times that narrate it.

Inner time: Lived experience

The personal sense of time is embodied and embedded, and therefore it tends to be at odds with the mechanical grid of time. While as human beings we are able to adjust to these ever-faster beats of social life, and even be fascinated by the sublime elements of the high speed and the large scale, we may also suffer from the sense of insecurity that is associated with such ephemerality. A discrepancy between the external stimuli and personal responses may be a permanent feature of this interface, as our biology and psychology, as well as our social and environmental contexts may not be so easy or ready to change, and in any such change our vulnerabilities may be heightened and be exposed. This part examines this interface, as seen from a first-person perspective, in subjective and intersubjective forms, as compared to the previous chapters that looked at temporality from a third-person and impersonal perspective.

The subjective experience of time is a central theme of phenomenology, considered by its founder, Edmund Husserl, to be 'its most important matter ... the most difficult of all phenomenological problems' (Brough, 1981:271). The focus of phenomenology was on experiences and their structure, and as the word suggests, it involved offering an account (logos) of what appears to us (phenomenon). Its aim was to provide an alternative approach that would contrast, and complement, the positivist account of the world, going beyond its natural attitude and its *a priori* and often unexamined assumptions. Largely embraced by natural scientists, positivism was a version of empiricism combined with logic and linguistics. It was based on investigating what could be observed and measured, thereby dismissing the subjective experience as irrelevant. Phenomenology, in contrast, was a search for an alternative approach that would take into account subjectivity and the role of the observer in the development of knowledge. It became a serious rival to positivism and the source of inspiration for a series of theoretical developments since the beginning of the twentieth century. The phenomenological analysis involved not the data from the real world but from a person's own mental experience; it therefore focused on the space of consciousness, that is, the way the world appeared to us, trying to develop an account that would be free from presuppositions. Like the Cartesian method, it was based on introspection. The aim of the analysis was to reveal the internal structure of what Husserl called the 'experiences of meaning' (Pivcevic, 1970:12).

Edmund Husserl (1981; 1991) focused on 'subjective time-consciousness', or the 'lived experience of time', which he contrasted with objective time. He argued that objective time, which could be grasped in an empirical experience, was not the focus of attention for his analysis; it needed to be suspended in a phenomenological analysis: 'world time, the real time, the time of nature in the sense of natural science' were not phenomenological data (Husserl, 1991:4–5). Inherent in the phenomenological analysis of time-consciousness was 'the complete exclusion of every assumption, stipulation, and conviction with respect to objective time' (Husserl, 1991:4). Instead, the attention was to be focused on our consciousness of temporal objects. Consciousness of time becomes a central feature of the lived experience: how temporal objects, for example a melody, appears to our consciousness: 'the time we assume is the *immanent* time of the flow of consciousness, not the time of the experienced world' (Husserl, 1991:5). The emphasis on an inner sense of time would offer an alternative understanding that would fundamentally differ from the mathematical calculations of the measured time. If objective time connected temporal fragments together through a measured grid, subjective time linked them to each other through consciousness and memory.

In the existentialist tradition that overlapped phenomenology, Heidegger shares Husserl's critique of the natural attitude, attacking science's mathematical and calculative thinking, as well as philosophy's traditional metaphysics based on a subject looking at an object. Instead, he advocates awareness of a self-concealed being becoming present to itself through disclosure, arriving at a presence that Heidegger calls being there. In this thinking, time and temporality occupied a crucial position, identified as the phenomenon in which 'the central problematic of all ontology' is rooted (Heidegger, 1962:40). Heidegger refers to 'interpreting Dasein as temporality' (Heidegger, 1962:38), and so he argues that 'Time must be brought to light – and genuinely conceived – as the horizon for all understanding of Being and for any way of interpreting it' (Heidegger, 1962:39). This is not the traditional concept of time that has persisted from Aristotle to Bergson and beyond, whereby temporal means being 'in time'; instead, temporality here means 'primordial time' (Heidegger, 1962:457) through which existence is lived and experienced. *Dasein* is a German word for existence, meaning 'to be here', an entity characterized by intentionality (Turetzky, 1998:183); it is Heidegger's ontological term for human beings (Pivcevic, 1970:110): 'we *are* it, each of us, we ourselves' (Heidegger, 1962:36).

Heidegger's main interest is to explore the meaning of being, which he found to be closely intertwined with temporality. He argues that 'The essence of Dasein lies in its existence' (Heidegger, 1962:42). This existence, and becoming aware of it, unfolds through time; it is disclosed with time. Time is not a sequence of nows, but a unifying factor for being-in-the world: 'Dasein exists outside its own present, carried away to its own future and past' uniting them through lived experience (Turetzky, 1998:187). It unfolds in relation to the milieu in which we live: 'Dasein tends to understand its own Being in terms of that being to which it is essentially, continually, and most closely related – the "world"' (Heidegger, 1978:18). Moods are the way this relationship with the world is experienced, and it is in the tension between the unity of experience and the differences of the moods that we can see how temporality both unites and fragments the ontological-existential experience of the world. The states of mind change, but, he argues, 'Anything which is observed to have the character of turning up and disappearing in a fleeting manner, belongs to the primordial constancy of existence' (Heidegger, 1978:390). In particular, the mood of anxiety reveals something essential about existence, as we are thrown into the world and ultimately face the end of our time. Temporality of existence means that it is always in transition, affected by what has been, projected into what is to become, and anxious about its limits and its end.

The problem of the phenomenological account was that, by avoiding the data from the common sense and locating the description of experience in introspection and consciousness, it had to address the problem of others. This was the unity and integration of the fragments for a single individual, but how could these be shared and mutually understood? We can describe the world and the sense of time from an individual point of view, whether empirical and common sense or phenomenological and interpretive. But how can the descriptions of two individuals be compared or mutually understood? Husserl's solution to this problem was the idea of lifeworld (Lebenswelt), the realm of everyday life in which we live and share ideas and experiences with others (Pivcevic, 1970). The possibility of a holistic and intersubjective account would therefore be provided in this shared realm of lived experience. Later, thinkers such as Alfred Schutz (1970) tried to overcome the problem of relating the internal and external views of the world through a marriage of sociology and phenomenology. This was a social solution to an epistemological problem. Others tried to avoid the gap between subjective and objective accounts altogether through developing synthetic approaches that would conceptualize time as multiplicity and becoming.

These critiques of quantified time aim to develop an alternative account through which the temporal experience can be understood and explained. Despite their differences, they tend to share some common ground. Their point of overlap is the sense of time as experienced and understood from a subjective standpoint, which unites the fragments of experience and brings together the past, present and future. The unity of these experiences is guaranteed within the state of consciousness by a transcendental self (Husserl), and a primordial existential experience (Heidegger). Describing the experience of temporality may find ever more complex metaphysical expressions that strive to articulate the sense of personal time, but what they share is the ambition to go beyond the empiricist and positivist accounts and the instrumental and technological ways of approaching time. Rather than describing time as numbers, which has been a prevalent approach, they describe it through experiences, images and words, thereby getting close to artistic ways of expression. This is why Heidegger moved into poetic methods of expression as the best way to understand and describe these experiences. If, however, the ambition is to avoid the fragmentation of temporality that objective time has created, how can the subjective standpoint be assessed for its success in providing a holistic account of temporality?

The overall direction of all these analyses, despite their differences, is to look for a way of understanding time that goes beyond mathematical calculations and mechanical measurement, and instead develop a deeper description of the experience of time as felt and understood by human beings. They acknowledge the idea of the public time as its general and common character: 'The measurement of time gives it a marked public character, so that only in this way does what we generally call "the time" becomes well known' (Heidegger, 1962:471). But they cannot be satisfied with the limitations that this public idea of time creates for the experience of time. While some analysts in this tradition are overtly anti-scientific, others try to show the subjective standpoint to be a companion rather than a rival to the objective account of time, or even trying to go beyond this dichotomous interpretation of time. Fragmented moments and events would therefore be either united through an external order that is described and measured through numbers, or they could be integrated and united through an internal sense of temporality.

Modernism emphasized the scientific approach to time, drawing heavily on a quantitative account of space and time. With its drive for radical functionalist transformation, it had caused ruptures in temporality that could no longer be justified during the periods of economic austerity and collective insecurity. The critique of the quantitative time, therefore, becomes particularly strong when modernism comes under attack for its shortcomings. The linear and sequential concepts of time had been embraced by the future-oriented optimism of modernism. All that was stable and secure was now being continually questioned on utilitarian and functional grounds. Modernization of all aspects of life meant that everything was continually open to change and transformation. By the last quarter of the twentieth century, however, this optimism had faded. These critical and subjective analyses of time that were based on lived experience provided an alternative to the reductionist ideas that modernism had promised and a respite from its pressure for continuous change that had rendered every aspect of life into a temporary performance. Rather than a progressive continuity, time would be conceptualized as interior and multiple, without any pre-determined direction of travel. In many ways, the rejection of modernist agenda and the emphasis on personal experience would open the door to a liberal conception of time that is non-essentialist and open for personal interpretation. Rather than an external order, time was ordered through an internal experience of consciousness. This was a critique of universalizing and accelerating modernity through introspection and localization.

Layered time

The idea of a single time that can be measured and accounted for faces a serious challenge when it comes to the social and historical time. The Enlightenment and the French Revolution changed the orientation towards time: modernity brought about a 'new time', which was accelerating and no longer a continuation of the past trends. What was new was 'a future that transcended the hitherto predictable' (Koselleck, quoted in Zammito, 2004:126). The radical openness and unpredictability of the new time 'abbreviated the space of experiences, robbed them of their constancy, and continually brought into play new, unknown factors' (Koselleck, quoted in Zammito, 2004:127). The only way that it could be accounted for was through belief in progress. In response, there was a recognition that time was multi-layered.

Historians write about a multi-layered time, in which several layers of time, with different origins and durations, are all present at the same time (Zammito, 2004). Rather than a single interpretation of linear time, which gives a prominent character to a period, there are many such times at any moment. Fernand Braudel distinguished between the short-term event, the mid-term trend and structures of the *longue durée*. At each moment, all these different times would coexist, generating a multi-layered temporality, and the problem was to see how these different layers relate to one another. Accelerated temporality made it difficult to write the history of the past: 'We encounter ruptures in our experience with a rapidity that was not registered by earlier centuries in the same manner. Therewith, historians face the task posed by modernity to recognize the total otherness of the past' (Koselleck, quoted in Zammito, 2004:133). This would equally make difficult the task of thinking about the future, as the condition of 'total otherness' would similarly apply to the future. The emergence of a heightened sense of temporariness, therefore, may be traced back to the rise of modernity in the eighteenth century, rather than a short-term trend that we are witnessing now. We are also dealing with multiple structures with manifold timescales, which makes it difficult to see temporary urbanism as a single rupture in the flow of time, but as the overlap of many temporal changes in numerous temporal layers.

The emphasis on subjectivity and individuality, meanwhile, has challenged the inner sense of time, as it has magnified its multiplicity. Since the beginning of urbanization, the make-up of urban populations has been characterized by their social, economic and cultural diversity. In the life of hunters and gatherers, small bands of people lived in limited territories. In the formation of the first cities, however, the surplus of agricultural production, and the necessity of providing a range of services for a concentrated population, opened up the possibility of new activities conducted by different groups of people. In agrarian cities, the diversity of population went hand in hand with the division of labour, whereby the tasks of farming, trade, crafts, administration, religion and defence created a structured diversity that could persist for centuries, institutionalized into rigid cultural frameworks. When the Industrial Revolution attracted large numbers of people to work in urban factories, these old structures were unsettled, the division of labour was changed and the extent of diversity was magnified. Although many were squeezed into the new role of industrial worker, the urban populations came from different towns and cities, with completely different backgrounds. Their relations to each other and to their new urban environment had to be largely invented.

The emergence of the global economy has now once again dismantled the former division of labour and its structures of similarity and difference, while creating and intensifying new forms of diversity. The city is not only attracting new people, it is also starting to acknowledge the existing differences between its own long-term inhabitants, which hitherto had been suppressed and ignored. Diversity of the population is not merely a reflection of the increased immigration to the city, but also a reflection of the break-up of the old structures of similarity, and realizing the extent of existing diversity in the current populations. There had been deep differences inside the urban population, which had perhaps existed for a long time, but never recognized. The modern sense of diversity, in contrast, identifies and expands on the real or imagined diversity of highly urbanized and individualized populations. The conceptual and institutional frameworks that had bound the populations together would be weakened or melting away under the conditions of increased inequality, intensified cultural diversity, flexible work and heightened mobility. In this context, multiplicity becomes the primary basis of social ontology.

In a highly diverse and individualized society, temporality is multiplied and fragmented. The old collective routines that ruled the society may no longer function, as each person may work to a different tempo. The globalized city becomes poly-rhythmic, with overlapping patterns of temporality, creating round-the-clock vibrancy. As individuals are encouraged to develop their own unique personality, as expressed through a specific pattern of habits and commodity consumption, the times of the city become multiple and diverse to unprecedented levels. As each individual is encouraged to act as an entrepreneur, searching for new opportunities and taking innovative steps, the multiple times of the city become even more short-lived and numerous. There may emerge as many temporal forms as there are urban inhabitants. Temporariness and temporal multiplicity become tightly intertwined, rather than being channelled through a mechanical grid. Time may appear to be no more than a series of unrelated events. Temporariness becomes an inherent condition for much of urban living. To confront this temporal multiplicity and the relative loss of the overarching frameworks of meaning, quantitative time is reasserted as the ultimate neutral structure on which all events can hang.

A question that should be asked here is whether this social multiplicity is sufficient to describe the urban condition. The classical liberal thought envisaged society as an agglomeration of individuals who needed to become free from the bonds of history and tradition, so as to follow their own desires. This fine-grained vision of society, however, is no longer tenable, as the presence of large players would change the rules of the game. Social ontology is at one level made of individuals with highly diverse characteristics, but at another level there are formations of power that shape the social ontology in many different ways. Public and private corporations, social classes, and cultural, religious and ethnic communities form a different map of power in society. The social ontology that would take these formations into account would not be as fine grained, with a reduced level of multiplicity and difference than the one envisaged in a society of different individuals. Multiplicity in society would mean different things at different levels. Neither the classical liberal concepts of free individuals in competition with each other nor the contemporary concept of social diversity would remain unchallenged by reality.

Temporal multiplicity

Henri Bergson has been considered to be the forerunner of phenomenology, albeit with significant differences. He conceptualized time as Durée, which he identified as heterogeneous, continuous and 'pure multiplicity' (Turetzky, 199). Bergson first identified Durée as consciousness, but he later broadened it to explore the unconscious memory, the existence of the past, the élan vital of creative evolution and the whole universe. Durée is not the same as consciousness, but can be intuitively accessible through consciousness, where it is disclosed as 'an enduring becoming' (Turetzky, 210). The key features of Durée are multiplicity and continuity. Two types of multiplicity are distinguishable: quantitative and qualitative. Quantitative multiplicity is the perspective of physics, assigning numbers to all matter and space, conceptualized as multiplications of homogeneous entities. By contrast, qualitative multiplicity, which is the realm of Durée, refers to the continuity of heterogeneous entities that are concrete and distinctive from one another, which therefore cannot be captured by numbers. Durée cannot be measured, as these multiple and successive entities are not the same and do not share the same identity. Durée is also continuous, but in this continuity it does not remain the same, as it changes qualitatively.

This temporal multiplicity is the result of a spatial distinction between different life trajectories embodied in different human beings. In a Bergsonian interpretation, it would be a spatial representation of temporal multiplicity. Henri Bergson identifies two types of multiplicity: spatial and temporal, accounted for by quantitative and qualitative means. As he writes, 'there are two kinds of multiplicity: that of material objects, to which the conception of number is immediately applicable; and the multiplicity of the states of consciousness, which cannot be regarded as numerical without the help of some symbolical representation, in which a necessary element is *space*' (Bergson, 2002:54). In thinking about time, we may tend to separate the moments from one another simultaneously and think about them as a succession of distinctive states. In this way, we have turned the temporal into the spatial, as it has been represented by a succession of distinguishable and separable states. According to Bergson, 'there are two possible conceptions of time, the one free from all alloy, the other surreptitiously bringing in the idea of space' (Bergson, 2002:60).

Bergson (2002:60) defines time in terms of duration, which is free of subdivision and quantitative representation: 'Pure duration is the form which the succession of our conscious states assumes when our ego lets itself *live*, when it refrains from separating its present state from its former states.' This concept of time is about 'succession without distinction ... a mutual penetration, an interconnection and organization of elements, each one of which represents the whole and cannot be distinguished or isolated from it except by abstract thought' (Bergson, 2002:60). If we had no idea of space, we would give such an account of duration, an account by 'a being who was ever the same and ever changing' (2002). But as we cannot avoid being spatial, our account of time also becomes spatial: 'we set our states of consciousness side by side in such a way as to perceive them simultaneously, no longer in one another, but alongside one another; in a word, we project time into space' (2002). When we speak of time as the order of duration, we have already spatialized time, as the development of an order would require distinguishing the elements from one another, setting them side by side simultaneously, comparing the places they occupy and introducing an order of succession.

Bergson, therefore, holds two types of multiplicity: 'actual multiplicities that are numerical and discontinuous and virtual multiplicities that are continuous and qualitative' (Deleuze, 1988:80). The ontological multiplicity of the city combines both forms of Bergsonian multiplicity: the intensifying diversity of individualized humans and the objects with which we live, which creates a spatial multiplicity, and the inherent and magnified diversity of our states of mind, which creates and magnifies temporal multiplicity. This would generate 'a radical plurality of durations' which go beyond psychological one: 'Psychological duration, our duration, is now only one case among others, among an infinity of others', where each duration has a rhythm of its own (Deleuze, 1988:76). After being faced with the theory of relativity, in which Einstein had used the concept of multiplicity, drawing on Riemann, however, it seems that Bergson had moved away from his notion of radical multiplicity and shifted his position towards temporal monism. He writes about 'a single

Time, one, universal, impersonal'; 'a single duration, in which everything would participate, including our consciousnesses, including living beings, including the whole material world' (Deleuze, 1988:78). He attempts to reconcile his ideas of temporal multiplicity and singularity through simultaneity, whereby different fluxes occupy the same duration in relation to 'internal duration, to real duration' (Bergson, quoted in Deleuze, 1988:81).

Whether or not the different concepts of time can be incorporated into a single concept of time, Einstein and Bergson share the idea of observer-dependent sense of time, where temporality revolves around the experiences of the observer. With the city being the gathering place of thousands and millions of such observers, its temporality is therefore made of thousands or millions of durations and fluxes, simultaneous and discordant, all experienced alongside one another. From a spatial perspective, these durations are all distinguishable from one another, and internally discontinuous, a series of short-lived events that are linked up internally through personal experience and externally through social narratives and public infrastructures of meaning. This would make temporary urbanism an inherent condition in the city at all times.

Following Bergson, Deleuze analyses time to have a double character: a present that contracts successive moments in a living present, and a compressed past that is always present; the former is material and actual and the latter is ideal and virtual. Deleuze calls this doubled presence to form a crystal of time (Turetzky, 1998:216). Inspired by Stoics, Deleuze distinguishes between an historical time (Chronos), in which events take place, where bodies and states of affairs are actualized, and an ahistorical time (Aion), which is the time of the event (Patton, 2010). Chronos is 'a living present' and measurable, while Aion is 'an incorporeal time' that cannot be measured (Turetzky, 1998:218–9), the realm of pure events, as the 'shadowy and secret part [of an event] that is continually subtracted from or added to its actualization' (Deleuze and Guattari, 1994:156). While history addresses Chronos, it cannot deal with 'the event in its becoming, in its specific consistency, in its self-positing concept' (Deleuze and Guattari, 1994:110). It is the task of philosophy to deal with Aion, producing concepts that express these pure events. Pure events are 'becoming itself, or the process by which something comes about', and therefore 'the condition of all change' (Patton, 2010:82). Following Nietzsche's idea of eternal recurrence, becoming is never stable and it always returns in different forms.

> It is no longer time that exists between two instants; it is the event that is a meanwhile *[un entre-temps]*: the meanwhile is not part of the eternal, but neither is it part of time – it belongs to becoming…. All the meanwhiles are superimposed on one another, whereas times succeed each other. In every

event there are many heterogeneous, always simultaneous components, since each of them is a meanwhile, all within the meanwhile that makes them communicate through zones of indiscernibility, of undecidability: they are variations, modulations, intermezzi, singularities of a new infinite order. (Deleuze and Guattari, 158)

Deleuze and Guattari's emphasis on becoming is a direct reminder of Nietzsche's way of thinking. In the relationship between being and becoming, Nietzsche rejects being and emphasizes becoming. 'What is real for Nietzsche is "becoming" – flux, multiplicity, change. Nietzsche uses many different terms to denote this flux ... But always the meaning is the same: becoming is restless primordial indetermination' (Houlgate, 1986:49). As Nietzsche (1989) set out to revalue all values, he looks for opening up new avenues in which these new values could be constructed. Rather than predetermined essences, and their associated fixed values, it is the course of life that determines its own meaning and value, as it unfolds in its multiplicity: 'that the world is no unity, either as sensorium or as 'mind', this alone is the great liberation – this alone re-establishes the innocence of becoming' (Nietzsche, quoted in Dries, 2008:115). In this radical emphasis on becoming, he comes close to the natural sciences, but also faced with the problem of continuity and identity:

And do you know what 'the world' is to me? Shall I show you it in my mirror? This world: an immensity of force, without beginning, without end, a fixed brazen quantity of force which grows neither larger nor smaller, which doesn't exhaust but only transforms itself ... as a play of forces and force-waves simultaneously one and 'many', accumulating here while diminishing there, an ocean of forces storming and flooding within themselves, eternally changing, eternally rushing back, with tremendous years of recurrence ... as a becoming that knows no satiety, no surfeit, no fatigue. (Nietzsche, quoted in Dries, 2008: 118–9)

The problem of the coexistence of qualitative temporal multiplicity alongside the continuity of identity is a problem that Alain Badiou tried to address. In his account of ontological multiplicity, Badiou (2005) separates multiplicity from change. At one level, he equates ontology with pure multiplicity, and thereby with mathematics. But he separates being from existence, mathematics from physics. A line of thought since Parmenides had emphasized the unity of existence. According to this line of thought, it is possible to separate a sensible level from an intelligible level of existence. Beyond what we can perceive with our senses, there is a higher level of being, which can only be grasped by intellect. This is a unitary basis of ontology. A rival line of thought since Heraclitus, meanwhile, had seen the world as no more than change and pure multiplicity, denying the existence of such unity. Badiou reaffirms ontological multiplicity, but he is faced with the problem of continuity of identity. How can a multiplicity change and remain the same? How can a human being change and remain the same? A multiplicity is defined by its constituent elements, and the only way to keep its identity is to stay the same rather than change. So for Badiou, being is multiplicity, equated with mathematics and unchanging, while existence is the condition of being in the world, equated with physics and submitted to change.

The idea of multiple times needs to encounter the modern concept of self. Alain Badiou argues that we live in 'a second epoch of the doctrine of subject' (Badiou, 2005:3). In the first epoch, a concept of the subject runs through from Descartes to Hegel, and becomes legible in Marx, Freud, Husserl and Sartre; it is the 'founding subject, centred and reflexive' (2005). The contemporary concept of the subject, in contrast, is 'void, cleaved, a-substantial, and ir-reflexive', whose existence can only be supposed in the context of particular processes (2005). With the two types of quantitative and qualitative multiplicity of temporality, we are faced with many individuals with many selves. The break-up of the temporal structure seems to be complete.

A paralysis of meaning may emerge that is unable to bridge the wide gaps generated by this dual multiplicity of subjects and subjectivities. What is the temporality of the multiple and hollow selves? If the self is a void experiencing multiple temporalities, and the world is made of temporal multiplicity, the powers of reified quantitative time inevitably take centre stage to arbitrate and connect these fragments together. An external structure, which is imbued with different sorts of political, economic and cultural power, rules over these temporal fragments. When the idea of the subject has been hollowed out, what happens to this diversity and multiplicity? Is there any possibility of originality and authenticity, or is it induced by the ready-made models of thought and behaviour such as the drive for consumption? What are the alternative ways that these temporal fragments can be linked to one another? Chapter 6 will explore the creative potentials of multiplicity.

Memory: Reconstructed time

The connective power of inner temporality relies on memory, unconscious and trace. The remains of the past, which have had significant meaning at the time of their construction, may have lost all their meaning, becoming objects of aesthetic contemplation, neglected and abandoned, or even demolished. By dramatic changes in the street patterns, skyline, place names and monuments, rapidly changing cities lose their connection to the past and their memories. In the absence of these connections, memories are invented and utilized for instrumental reasons, as exemplified by city marketing, encouraged by tourism and global competition. The multiple layers of time and the traces of the past, however, are combined to resist the pressure for social fluidity and the loss of memory, even if they are also reinterpreted and remade according to the new circumstances. The city's unconscious survives in traces, which include objects, beliefs and practices.

Modernism transformed the idea of time in the city, from a natural attitude in which buildings and places followed one another in an historical sequence to a calculative and comprehensive attitude that could envisage time as a consistent singularity. All the various elements that constituted the city were now brought together in a single scheme, which would move from now on according to an orderly beat. The modernist vision foresaw a final spatial configuration as the ideal urban form based on rational general principles. The critics of modernism looked instead to history as a source of cultural codes that could offer continuity without closing the door to novelty and diversity.

One of these critics was Aldo Rossi who looked for permanence in the city to confront the threat of temporal fragmentation that modernism had encouraged. For Rossi (1982), the concepts of locus, monument and type offer opportunities to articulate this sense of permanence. In this vision, places and locations persist and monuments are continually under construction, and while elements change their types will stay the same. As a result, continuity and rational predictability are guaranteed through continuous construction to invent and reinvent the city, in a recurring play of these types around the monuments and in stable locations. In a process of architectural design that Rossi (1982:18) calls analogy, 'elements are preexisting and formally defined, but whose true meaning is unforeseen at the beginning and unfolds only at the end of the process'. This is the architecture of rational principles, empirical multiplicity of singular artefacts and permanent recurrence. In the flux of the city, Rossi searches for enduring elements, which he finds in the monuments. Whereas the urban dynamics are expressed in destruction, demolition and change of use, monuments are the primary elements, fixed points that offer permanence, 'signs of the collective will as expressed through the principles of architecture' (Rossi, 1982:22) (Figure 4.1).

The main characteristics of Rossi's urban artefacts are imagination and collective memory, as Maurice Halbwachs (1992) had articulated and as Christine Boyer (1996) has reiterated. For Rossi (1982:41), type is 'the very idea of architecture, that which is closest to its essence'. He defined the concept of type as, 'something that is permanent and complex, a logical principle that is prior to form and that constitutes it' (Rossi, 1982:40). The housing types, for example, have not changed since the antiquity, even if the ways of living have. Type is not repeated like a model, but it finds different manifestations at each recreation. Inspired by de Saussure's structuralism (Rossi, 1982:22),

FIGURE 4.1 *Through the persistence of its monuments and institutions, the city has been named 'eternal' (Rome, Italy).*

he saw the city as a permanent structure that would fundamentally stays the same despite the change of its elements through time: 'the city is something that persists through its transformations, and that the complex or simple transformations of functions that it gradually undergoes are moments in the reality of its structure' (Rossi, 1982:55–6).

The sense of time that is inherent in consciousness is largely shaped through an interaction with the surrounding environment. The memories of this environment are one of the vehicles of helping to cope with the various changes that the temporal beats of the city bring about. A degree of familiarity and continuity is essential for the feeling of well-being, even for those who live a nomadic life. Indeed, it is in the context of familiarity that nomadism and freedom from the rigid conventions make sense. This suggests that familiarity and change are interdependent and one cannot exist without the other. They are two sides of the same coin: change would only make sense in the context of familiarity, and familiarity would only be welcome in the context of change. When one side dominates the equation and rules the other out, the conditions become too difficult to cope with. When the urban conditions freeze and citizens are stuck in unfair and unwelcome circumstances, they strive for positive change. On the other hand, the faster paces of life are confronted by the need for a degree of continuity and familiarity. The two positions of familiarity and change, and the senses of stability/stagnation or instability/transformation that follow, are all positions along a long spectrum, rather than fixed dualities.

This is particularly evident in the rapidly changing cities, where streets, buildings, monuments or shops and even street names change continuously, in places where in large-scale urban development projects or in piecemeal but accelerated change some residents are pushed out or relocated in the name of improvement or in the name of inevitable logic of the market. In these places, the experience of the citizens is that of disconnection and loss (Figure 4.2). They look for something familiar, so that they can cope with change. Especially if this change is the result of someone else's decisions, rather than their own choices, they find it difficult to accept or to come to terms with such unwanted change. When they move to a new area by choice, meanwhile, they would search for new routines, people and places that can become familiar through everyday encounters. They may also look to be connected to old familiarities that are still part of their lives. Many of the institutions of the modern life offer this familiarity: the same social class, the same chain stores, the same brands, the same newspapers and service providers can be found across different cities or even countries, making life in new places familiar enough.

FIGURE 4.2 *In rapidly changing cities, streets, buildings, monuments and even names change continuously, causing a sense of disconnection from the past (Tehran, Iran).*

However, even when a city changes beyond recognition, it still keeps some of its old characters in a kind of unconscious realm, through small traces that are left here and there, and in habits and routines, concepts and beliefs that people carry with them and share in their social life. Without being visible, this unconscious realm maintains a degree of continuity in society, even when the city's physical fabric and its social institutions have significantly changed. It is easy to find the streets that are centuries if not millennia old, whether or not we are aware of them; words and beliefs that we may share with our predecessors, even when we think that we live a thoroughly modern life; genes that we share with our distant ancestors, even when we think we have broken all bridges to the past. These fragments may come to our consciousness if we happen to know them, or to remember them, or to learn them through research or accidental encounter. Chains of familiarity and continuity may be broken through relentless and accelerated change, but memory, even in its fragments and invisible forms, in hidden traces and in overt remains of the past, attempts to keep a line of continuity.

In a sense, the city is only made up of temporary events, in a sequence of change that is fragmented or connected, slowing down and accelerating at all times. A series of processes link these fragments: public conventions, such as measured time, which place them all within an overall framework; personal experiences such as the bodily experiences and states of consciousness, which link up these fragments in an inner framework; and social practices such as mythologies, stories and intersubjective encounters that assign meaning to these fragments in many different forms.

Identity: Narrated time

Memory and identity are intertwined. Old certainties were reflected in the symbols that no longer communicate with the urban populations, who in turn now rely on fleeting symbols and digital frameworks of communication to construct multiple and provisional identities. Changing narratives, consumption and lifestyles and the visual culture all reflect the fluidity and multiplicity of cultural identities. Meanwhile, resistance to acceleration and fluidity is shown in movements such as slow food, slow cities and cloned towns, as well as in regressive politics of identity, in search of a local identity that can be placed against globalization, modernity and loss of local distinction (Hobsbawm, 1990; Anderson, 1991; Castells, 1996).

The loss of identity in the age of globalization is a major topic of debate, discussing how cities and localities across the world are increasingly variations on the same theme, where people apparently behave in the same way and consume the same goods and services, and are subject to the same global institutions and corporations. This has caused much anxiety about the emergence of 'clone cities', giving rise to the idea of asserting local identity as a form of resistance to globalizing forces. Identity, therefore, finds a crucial role in the cultural and political life of a place. However, cities are historical collections of objects and people, material and social facts, institutions and memories, whose identities across time and space are always multiple and contested by the process of change and representations of change. Identity cannot be easily pinned down, or be reduced to its visual qualities. Is loss of identity only to be equated with loss of distinctiveness and visual diversity, or is there more to the notion of place identity? How do we make sense of the notion of city identity? How can we work out a theoretical framework with which to think about identity, in particular about the identity of cities? In what ways can a focus on memory and identity help us analyse temporary urbanism?

The main argument here is that a city's identity lies in its relations of similarity and difference with other places and times, that is, how it resembles other places as well as its unique and continuous features that could give it a relatively stable sense of itself, and how, and by whom, this sense is narrated and change is managed (Madanipour, 2009; 2013). Identity is a narrative told from one perspective, and therefore, to understand this narrative, we need to understand the nature, dimensions and representations of change. Anxiety about identity rises when the pace and size of change seem to be beyond control. As evident from the fast growing urban areas around the world, now or in the past, in the developed and developing worlds, we see signs of concern about social stability and environmental quality. The ability to have some control over the substance, pace and representations of change is, therefore, essential for a city's inhabitants to have some sense of security in their identity. This would show the significance of a democratic process for managing this change. The role of temporary events would then be defined in relation to this sense of control: who is in charge, at what pace of change and with what intentions? Who initiates and who runs the temporary events, and what narratives do these events convey?

Many cities are a testimony to a long history.[1] If we stand on the riverside in Newcastle upon Tyne, for example, we can look around and see the remnants of two thousand years of history (Figure 4.3). What is now called Swing Bridge has replaced a Roman bridge over the river Tyne, a node on the wall that the emperor Hadrian built to protect his northernmost territories from the ancestors of the Scots. The straight and long streets such as Westgate Road are built along the wall, which ended in Wallsend further east. From this vantage point, we can see the Castle Keep, which was built a millennium

---

[1] This part of the chapter is a revised version of Madanipour (2013:49–63).

FIGURE 4.3 *Many layers of history are detectable in an urban landscape, with traces and memories from each period (Newcastle, UK).*

ago after William conquered Britain and built many castles to dominate the country. We can see the remains of the medieval walls and streets of the city, and buildings from medieval, Georgian, and Victorian periods, as well as the twentieth and twenty-first centuries. From our vantage point, they are all episodes in the past, all traces of ideas and practices that we may no longer recognize.

What we grasp in a 360-degree panorama has been in the making for two millennia. Each building, bridge and road has had an impact on the city, introducing a new element into an existing context. Two particular tensions can be easily visible on Newcastle quayside. One is the dramatic range of bridges that cross the river. They show how through the changing technologies of transport from the nineteenth century onwards, the ancient low-level crossing lost its role to the high-level railways, motor cars and metro. This change took over the medieval city, turning the riverside into a place of industry, a backyard to the city that was growing uphill. A new pedestrian bridge, however, shows a new life for the riverside. With the decline of the industries, buildings were abandoned and the quayside was turned into a rusty no-go area. As regeneration activities in the last thirty years have brought these areas back to life, people have moved back to the river for work or leisure. Some industrial buildings have remained, and some have been converted to new uses. But most have been erased, to make way for the new entertainment and work places that have changed and gentrified the character of the riverside. The city once moved away from the river, and has now partially returned there. In the process, many tensions have arisen, many lives flourishing or wasting. A combination of economic and technological change transformed the city that had grown before at the meeting point of a hill and a river, resulting in a city that bears features of all of its historic periods to varying degrees.

Like all long-established cities, Newcastle is formed of a multiplicity of temporal layers; each layer consists of a large number of objects and institutions developed during a different historical period. As new generations emerge, and the city goes through cycles of growth and decline, only some elements are left from each period, by chance or by design. As its layers have multiplied, the city today is more complex than ever before. Like all other complex phenomena, the difficulty is how to represent the city. On the one hand, this is a city that has survived the test of time, has continued to be a major city for a long period of time, and at least for the past one thousand years has had a continuity of name and identity. On the other hand, this is a city that has changed beyond recognition, and apart from a few elements, there is not much that can compare this city to its previous periods. Each element of the city may be associated with many readings, from past memories to contemporary meanings, all potentially coexisting in pieces of stone. When confronted by this multiplicity and complexity, the question is, how do we analyse the city and represent it? How do we account for a complex historical phenomenon that has gone through so many changes?

A traditional way of analysing the complexity of urban form has been urban morphology, which draws on historical geography (Conzen, 1960; Whitehand, 1987). The urban form is divided into three elements of street pattern, building form and land use. Each element is changing according to a different logic, which is somewhat in line with Braudel's three layers of historical time. So the land use may change from one day to the next, depending on how people decide to use a particular place. Building form is more resilient to change, as buildings have a longer life, which may last for generations, and even centuries. Once built, a particular building form is likely to remain more or less the same for a longer period of time, while the use of that building may change several times. The third element, the street pattern, is the most resilient, as it can remain unchanged for centuries. In many European city centres, medieval street layouts can be identified. In some cities the Roman street patterns have persisted. In this way, the many layers of the city can be analysed into functions and types, to see how the city is a tapestry of physical elements from different ages, woven together through the overlapping of different textures and threads. As urban morphologists have shown, it is then possible to identify character areas in the city, where the streets and buildings may be traced back to a particular historic period.

This is a descriptive analysis of the physical environment, to link its complexity to different historic periods. But when it comes to the modern day, we need more complicated tools that can explain the current dimensions of change. We also need a tool that would enable us to connect the physical and social environment of the city, and its present to its past and future. The city's social environment is also formed of many layers, embedded in its particular norms and habits, its local use of language, its own history of people and events, its institutions and its memories.

Identity across space

We often hear complaints about the loss of identity in a place, where rapid development and lack of attention to the quality of development have produced a bland environment. Modernist redevelopments of historic cities are thought to deprive them of their character, while many new parts of cities are criticized for their inability to claim any sense of identity. Globalization is thought to be creating pressures for homogeneity and loss of local character and identity. From these accounts, it would appear that the loss of identity is equated with reduction in difference. The question then becomes about the distinctive features of a city: What distinguishes one city from another? What is unique about it? Increasingly, the response has been the establishment of iconic features and complicated marketing strategies to discover, or invent, new markers. Cities are treated as goods on the shelves of supermarkets, hence the significance of product differentiation, the need for standing out in a crowded marketplace. Temporary urbanism, when developed to create these marketable distinctions, may be seen to be part of the same phenomenon of seeking difference in a global competition.

Identity, however, is not only about distinction. It also deals with features that are similar to others. Here we can draw on social philosophy's definition of identity, which sees social identity as the result of the relations of similarity and difference (Jenkins, 1996). Individuals define their identity by defining who they are similar to, and who they are different from. The same can be seen in cities and their parts. How can a city be similar to, and different from other cities?

Relations of similarity often take place within similar cultural and historical contexts. We can talk about medieval European cities, or medieval Middle Eastern cities, where the internal interactions of a civilization would lead to similarities among its cities. We can, therefore, identify a city as belonging to a group of cities with similar features. The identity of the city, therefore, is partly based on its similarities. But even within a relatively homogeneous context such as the medieval cities, we will see unique features. The best examples are Gothic churches: whereas they all belong to the same European cultural, geographical and historic context, they are all different. Each city has applied the same set of ideas in a different context, with different combinations of architectural elements; the result is diversity as well as unity. Each city has tried to stand out by virtue of its greatest artefact, while using the same alphabet to stress its similarities with others like it (Figure 4.4).

In the modern period, this question is often raised in reaction to worldwide styles such as functionalism, which seemed to promote a universal pattern across the world, and which appeared to be turning cities to be similar everywhere, eroding local and regional distinctions. With globalization, this concern has intensified. What is a locality's identity in the face of homogenizing forces of globalization? Large companies that work across national boundaries, global networks of information and communication, and intensified movement of people, resources, goods, services and ideas have contributed to the emergence of global patterns of similarity.

The way the constituent parts of a city are shaped and related to one another creates a unique identity for that city, which makes it identifiable from other cities. By the emergence of global brands, retail chains, multinational corporations, and international styles of architecture and urban design, the distinctiveness of cities is being eroded. However, psychological well-being of people in localities seems to require the establishment of some

FIGURE 4.4 *Within a shared culture, each city has tried to stand out by the construction of its greatest artefact (Cologne, Germany).*

distinctive character. This is why a heightened attention to memorable objects, institutions and events has emerged. In the past, public buildings such as museums and libraries, or private ones such as skyscrapers, were erected as monuments by cities which had the necessary wealth and ambition. Now, flagship projects, football clubs and festivals are some of the devices that help establish a relationship of similarity and difference with other cities. The current competition for erecting the tallest building in the world, in cities such as Taipei, Kuala Lumpur, Dubai, London and New York, shows that the concern for status has been intensified. The struggle for status, as argued by Weber and Bourdieu, is a driving force in society. Status secures not only a cultural sense of uniqueness; it also fuels a sense of economic competitiveness in a global economy that has become increasingly interconnected.

The sense of uniqueness and status has a clear economic logic: claiming to belong to an elite set of cities which can hope to play the part of a node in the global economy. Iconic architecture is not merely a sign of cultural and social distinctions, but also a sign of economic similarity, bidding for the membership of an elite club. Even when cities bid for distinction, therefore, they are asserting a relation of similarity at the same time. Local authorities decide who they wish to compete with, set them as benchmarks and try to find out what they have done to succeed. If our competitors have a Zaha Hadid, Norman Foster or Frank Gehry building, so should we (Figure 4.5). If

FIGURE 4.5 *Icons are used to project a distinctive identity, by reference to extraordinary height, unusual shape and the global brand of the architect (Glasgow, UK).*

they have a world expo, a garden festival and an international art event, so should we. If they have street art, glitzy public spaces and open-air leisure and entertainment, so should we. If they have pop-up restaurants and temporary buildings, so should we. This is a process in which differentiation is desired, but assimilation may be the outcome. A sense of identity is established through the relations of similarity and difference. These relations, however, are not only across space, but also over time.

Identity over time

The problem of a city's identity has some similarity to the classical philosophical problem of personal identity over time. How is it possible that, over a period of time, a person remains the same? Is it through physical continuity, or psychological persistence, or both, that a person's identity over time is established (Olson, 2002)? As discussed earlier in this chapter, the plurality of the selves, both in their spatial diversity and temporal multiplicity, would undermine this sense of continuity. The same questions can be posed about cities. How do we say that a city is the same as it was three a generation ago or century ago? Is it through the persistence of its physical elements? Or is it through the memories and feelings of its inhabitants that the city keeps its identity? Or is it a combination of both? But there is no single account for these interpretations, and so the questions become: What are the accounts of the physical and social-psychological continuities, and whose account is acceptable and by whom?

There are, however, some important differences between the notion of personal identity and the collective identity of a city. In the case of individuals, the physical body may change over time, but it remains a single unit which ages and transforms. The city may stay in the same location or have the same name, but it is formed of many people and objects, which change according to different patterns and paths, and are interpreted by different people and at different times. While some grow old, others are renovated. The result is a complex set of objects and relationships that are constantly evolving, with many possible and competing identities, as seen from different perspectives.

One of the problems of identity over time is the distinction between body and mind: is it the body's persistence over time that constitutes identity, or is it the psychological continuity that is the ground for identity? The general attitude seems to prefer psychological continuity as the basis of identity. However, in cities, this will be more complicated than in personal identity. If we take the psychological approach, we soon realize that memories are about people as well as about places. The mental states that determine identity are, therefore, not self-referential, but intentional, directing towards outside events and objects.

The way personal identity is analysed appears to draw on dualism of mind and body. In the modern period, the ancient dualism between the mind and the body was reaffirmed by Descartes, and hence has since been called Cartesian dualism (Cottingham, 1992a). He argued that the mind (or soul) is non-physical and is distinct from the body or other material objects: '... this 'I', that is to say, the mind, by which I am what I am, is entirely distinct from the body' (Descartes, 1968:54). This gave him a solid rational foundation for knowledge, which was thinking: 'I think, therefore I am' (Descartes, 1968:53). This separation has been challenged by later generations, to the extent that now most philosophers consider themselves anti-Cartesian in this respect, adopting a kind of materialism which integrates the mind and the body (Cottingham, 1992b; Searle, 1999; Žižek, 1999). Psychoanalysts have argued that the body can influence the mind (Freud, 1985), and neuroscientists have shown a two-way traffic between the brain and the body, and how the way people behave can change if their brains are damaged, hence challenging the divide (Greenfield, 2000).

By separating the social from the physical dimensions of the city, we are in danger of applying a version of dualism to the city (Figure 4.6). By asking whether the city is what it is due to its material objects, or to the people who live there, we are using Cartesian dualism to analyse the city. Identity, therefore,

FIGURE 4.6 *Separating the social and physical dimensions applies a reductionist and dualistic concept to the city (Glasgow, UK).*

is not entirely about the physical or entirely about the social continuity, but it is often a combination of the two. If we move new people to an old city, of which they know nothing, as for example after bloody conquests, can we talk about the continued identity of the place? On the other hand, if we move the people of a city to a new location, for example rebuilt after a disaster or a major urban renewal scheme, can we talk about their continued identity? Are they the citizens of the same city, or of a new city? In both cases, a new set of relationships will be gradually established between people and places, and a new identity for the city will emerge.

Interrupted identities in the age of speed

Cities are large agglomerations of people and objects. At any moment in time, some of these constituent parts of the city are changing: babies are born, new people come to the city, new roads and buildings are built, but also some people leave, old people die and ageing buildings are demolished. It would be impossible to imagine a living city without these changes. In the short term, these small changes cannot have a major impact on the city as a whole; a complete change of the city does not take place. Over time, however, the accumulated effects of these changes may largely change the city. In extreme cases of change, the city, and even its memory, may be wiped out altogether.

This slow historical change seems to be expected as part of the natural cycle of human settlements. Problems emerge, however, when the pace of change is fast and its dimensions large. Many European cities grew in the nineteenth century as a result of industrialization. The speed of urban growth in Victorian Britain was so alarming that many of the elite were worried about the possible impact of this growth on the future of society (Briggs, 1968). The anxiety and fear that accompanied the urban growth led to many efforts to instigate new forms of solidarity, whether based on religion, on tradition, on collective work or on associations (Durkheim, 1972a). Similarly, some of the anxieties of the past thirty years can be attributed to the large-scale move out of the industrial era. Cities that were once the seat of industries started to lose their functions and rationale. The Newcastle quayside is the prime example of these changes of entry into and out of industrial period. Urban growth now accompanies anxieties for the degradation of environment and quality of living of places. In the United States, the pace of growth, particularly in fast-growing sunbelt areas such as Arizona or California, has troubled the city authorities who are interested in managing this change, but are unable to keep up with its pace.

In the developing world, urban growth is often phenomenal. The pace and dimensions of change are such that the authorities seem unable to cope with its demands. A new infrastructure of roads, schools, hospitals, etc., is needed to serve the urban growth. However, the financial and institutional capacities of the local or national authorities are limited. The pace of change also worries the urban middle classes, who feel their safety and security are under threat. Gated neighbourhoods from China to South Africa to the United States are developed on the basis of an argument for safety and security. The use of public space for informal trade is a prime example of temporary urbanism by the poor in many cities around the world. Here ephemerality is a sign of economic weakness, an attempt to cope with the lack of jobs and the inability of the authorities and their regulations to control the development and use of urban space. Temporariness of the street trades is a challenge to an ineffective political and economic system (Babere, 2013). Temporary urbanism also reflects extreme forms of vulnerability such as tent cities and refugee camps set up after natural disasters and wars, or the informal settlements of the poor (Figure 4.7).

The pace of change threatens the sense of identity that urban societies have, especially in the age of globalization, when the pace of change has intensified. This has been felt in Western cities, where the international styles of architecture and the spread of international goods and services have produced ever more similarity than before. This has been more strongly felt in the developing world, where these international symbols have had the dual

FIGURE 4.7 *Informal settlements signify the extent of precarity and the condition of temporary existence for many people around the world (Johannesburg, South Africa).*

character of modernity and loss of identity and control, ideas imported from abroad that signal a desirable change that keeps us in line with the rest of the world, as well as taking control of our destiny further away from us.

Powerful players are able, with the help of new technologies, to move ideas, resources, goods and services around the world at ever-faster speeds. This has speeded up social processes and routines. Technological change has transformed social behaviour, creating a fast pace of life, faster than ever before. However, there are objects around us that constantly remind us of the longer scales of time, a sense of continuity that defies the speed of social life. Astronomical and geological times are extremely long range, measured in millions and billions of years, even light years, which are beyond our grasp and even imagination. And yet these long spans can be observed in humble pieces of stone that we see around us everywhere. A sense of permanence can be detected in the building materials that we use to build our cities.

Artefacts bring with them a measure of permanence and durability to human life and at the same time condition human existence. '[H]uman existence', Hannah Arendt wrote, 'is conditioned existence, it would be impossible without things, and things would be a heap of unrelated articles, a non-world, if they were not the conditioners of human existence' (Arendt, 1958:9). The integration of humans and things in the construction of public space endows the public realm with permanence. As Arendt (1958:55) wrote:

> Only the existence of a public realm and the world's subsequent transformation into a community of things which gathers men together and relates them to each other depends primarily on permanence. If the world is to contain a public space, it cannot be erected for one generation and planned for the living only; it must transcend the life-span of mortal men.

In this way the world of artefacts not only mediates between the present members of the public, it also links them to other generations through time. This integration of people and objects in the analysis, and the appreciation of how social relations are mediated through objects, is a key point in Arendt's analysis of public space. Objects and relations, however, may lose their meaning from one period to another. The connection will be reduced to a trace, hinting at an unconscious life of the city that could only be discovered through archaeology. There are others after Arendt who have attempted to integrate people and objects, although some have gone as far as giving the objects a degree of agency in social processes (Latour, 1993). The significance of objects is indeed dependent on a process of collective symbolization, in which we allocate meaning to objects and events (Searle, 1995).

The historical scale is much faster than astronomical and geological scales, and yet slower than technological and social changes. Much of the city, particularly its old parts and historical monuments, remains the same even after decades of rapid change in social habits and technological innovation. We may use computers in medieval buildings, without feeling uneasy about the discrepancy. These old objects, places and buildings are signs of a relative permanence, defying the speed that dominates social life. In this capacity, they can reassure the citizens that there are some focal points that remain constant, even if everything else changes. Even at the social scale of daily life, speed is being resisted. The Slow Food movement, for example, which boasts over 80,000 members in 100 countries, came into being in 1986 with the aim of protecting 'the pleasures of the table from the homogenization of modern fast food and life' (Slow Knox, 2005; Food, 2006). Rather than returning to traditional methods of agriculture and agrarian forms of life, Slow Food and Slow City movement uses modern technologies but argues for an alternative pace of life. It aims to slow down the imposed acceleration of global time while emerging as a brand that would distinguish cities in a global marketplace. The networks of slow food and slow city help their members be part of a movement of similarity while generating a sense of distinction. They are a movement of identity formation with economic and social implications in a globalizing world (Figure 4.8).

FIGURE 4.8 *The Slow Food movement, born in places like the City of Bra, near Turin, is a form of resistance to temporal acceleration caused by the globalizing effects of fast food (Bra, Italy).*

Dynamic multiplicity: Many voices, over time

Identity is established through the relations of similarity and difference, but it crucially depends on the process of representation of these relations. There are many disparate elements in anyone's memory, and the way they are brought together to make sense of their experiences is through the narrative that is told for oneself or others. Personal identity, therefore, is considered to be a narrative identity (Ricoeur, 1995). The way I establish the relations of similarity and difference to my own past and to others is through telling stories, describing the elements of continuity and disruption, my similarities with and differences from others, and looking for social recognition in return (Honneth, 1995). A human being, however, has a complex memory and a large mental capacity. Which features of my past do I remember or should I choose to compare to my present? Which features of my mental and physical make-up should I choose to compare to others? These elements all go through a process of selection, consciously and unconsciously, resulting in a narrative that is at best selective and partial, and subject to change from time to time. Many elements of this identity remain untold, until the moment that a contrary narrative is produced, which may appear to undermine the underlying assumptions and hidden features which may not even be known to the person until that moment of contradiction. A similar process can be observed in the representation of cities and societies.

A city is a complex and multi-layered spatial-temporal phenomenon. Which features are adopted as symbols with which to specify and describe a place? Under the conditions of rapid change and ephemeral circumstances, which stories can last long enough to be told? Which stories remain untold and hidden and which stories are found to be contradictory and threatening? This is closely related to the question of who is the agent in charge of this selection and description, and the methods of narration and representation. Through different representations, we may hear completely different stories about a place. The process of representation is thwarted by a multitude of problems and contestations. One problem is the selection of symbols with which to identify a place. Here the problem of stereotyping looms large. How do we describe a people? This often takes place through ineffective and prejudiced symbolization, as famously exemplified in national and regional stereotypes. But if we look from within these communities, we may not recognize the stereotype at all. The other problem is a political one: who tells the story and to what end?

In both manifestations of identity, through time and across space, the question remains as to which elements of the city is chosen to represent its distinctive features. In the case of individuals, deciding who we are similar to and different from is a process that mixes real and imaginary features, creating a social construct that is often contested but also necessary for the psychological well-being of individuals. As individuals are pulled in different directions – on the one hand by biological impulses and on the other hand by the social pressures for conformity – they develop a mask, a stable appearance that they use in social encounters (Goffman, 1969). Even though these pressures may be inscribed on their body as their character and so difficult to change (Bourdieu, 2000), they try to wear a mask that would hide what they consider as weak, choosing the best appearance that they wish to show to others (Madanipour, 2003).

As the city is a place of diverse people and physical spaces, the choice of what to represent is fairly open. To avoid essentialism, we cannot rely on a single narrative and a rigid identity to describe all these differences. The result would inevitably be multiple and dynamic identities, changing over time and across space, not only in relation to other places and periods, but also to the city's present time and space. Even here and now, we can find these differences that need to be included in an account of the city. The reality of the city, therefore, is always multiple and, depending on the narrator, we can hear different stories about its identity.

Nevertheless, we come across representations of the city all the time. Some of these are targeting particular audiences. For example, city marketing, which has become one of the main forms of competition in the global economy, puts forward a promotional profile for a city or a region, with the aim of attracting investors and visitors. Some fiction writers have presented cities in a specific light, so that there are themed visitors who search for the places mentioned in their novels, as for example tourists searching for the Da Vinci Code in Paris, or Inspector Rebus in Edinburgh. Heritage trails go through cities in a particular order, to tell a historical story or to take visitors through the main tourist attractions, as exemplified in Boston. City maps show places that are likely to be interesting for visitors, and edit other places out. Depending on who has provided the map, the locations will be shown with different emphases, as for example the map of Paris by Printemps department stores. Histories of cities are similarly coloured by the choices that the historian makes: what stories are told and for whom, which periods are considered to be more important and which characters need to be introduced. What are thought to be the causal relations would determine the instrumental uses of representation.

From a mass of information, there is always a careful selection of stories and symbols to tell a particular story about a city's past or present. These would amount to a wealth of material and a richer profile for a city. Tensions, however, may arise if people disagree on a profile. What city marketing material presents may be at odds with the realities, as well as hopes and desires, of local communities. The act of representation, however, gives the provider a degree of power, to tell the story in the way that may serve their aims, which may be exclusionary towards others.

These are relatively softer forms of representation. When they are turned into buildings and streets, they become strongly embedded in a place, and any change may become difficult. Over centuries, city centres have become the place over which powerful people and institutions have struggled to control and shape. By placing a church at the centre of the medieval European city, the control of the city's representation has been clearly given to an institution. By building high-rise towers at the heart of the American city, representation has been secured for the business elite. Accumulation of these controls has created an urban landscape, especially at the centre of cities, which is a map of power, and how the powerful have stamped their mark on the city, ensuring that its representation bears their presence. Temporary events, in one sense, can challenge these representations, offering an alternative reading of a place; alternatively, they can accompany and consolidate these forms of power by adding flavour and flexibility to their representation and the experience of the city.

Many critics of globalization, or of the fast pace of urban change, write about identity. For them, cultural identity appears to be a form of resistance to the fast movement that is transforming the familiar landscapes and norms of localities (Castells, 1996). Cultural identity becomes an instrument of injecting a degree of fixity into what appears to be fluid, ever changing and beyond our control. And yet we know that this fixity is in danger of becoming too rigid, rejecting the possibility of change that is needed for social vitality, and the possibility of change through dialogue with others. Rigid interpretations of cultural identity, as something essentially the same and unchanging, however, can lead to forms of intolerant tribalism. Some have celebrated this tribalism as a route to social renewal (Maffesoli, 1996), but the consequences of heightened tribalism are now increasingly apparent in multicultural societies. As discussed earlier, social identity is a process, which systematically establishes and signifies the relationship of similarity and difference between individuals, between collectivities, and between individuals and collectivities (Jenkins, 1996). Therefore, it is both through similarity and difference, and allowing for the possibility of change, that identity can be interpreted and understood.

Rather than a static understanding of space from a single perspective, or an abstract understanding of time, we need to be able to draw on different perspectives, and combine an understanding of time and space together. Dynamic multiplicity, therefore, is an investigation of the city through time and through the different perspectives of embedded and embodied agents interacting with each other and with their physical environment (Madanipour, 2007). It is crucial that the process of giving an account and accepting one is not one simple exchange, but an ongoing conversation, which can only be successful if a critical conversation is possible. As J.S. Mill insisted, human wisdom could only result from the 'steady habit of correcting and completing his own opinion by collating it with those of others' (Mill, 1974:80). This required an environment that guaranteed the freedom of expression and recognized that the truth may have many sides: 'the only way in which a human being can make some approach to knowing the whole of a subject is by hearing what can be said about it by persons of every variety of opinion, and studying all modes in which it can be looked at by every character of mind' (1974). Nietzsche says almost the same, but in his own words. He warns us that any rational analysis is an interpretation from a viewpoint, but to counter the effects of entrapment in a single perspective, Nietzsche suggests we 'employ a *variety* of perspectives and effective interpretations in the service of knowledge' (quoted in Schacht, 1996:159). As he puts it, 'the *more* affects we allow to speak about one thing, the *more* eyes, different eyes, we can use to observe one thing, the more complete will our "concept" of this thing, our "objectivity", be' (1996). Therefore, a multidimensional viewpoint is required, which draws on different perspectives, integrating political, economic and cultural aspects of urban transformation. This viewpoint needs to be dynamic, so that it can address the process of urban change: incorporating a time dimension into the process of spatial change, rather than only focusing on a particular place or a single moment in this process. Ultimately, however, its role is not just mapping the diversity of views, but also showing what may be missing, what has remained unsaid, making visible what often remains invisible.

Conclusion

The quantitative concepts of time are used to construct a social grid which frames, controls and accelerates social life. This social grid is the way the fragments of events are pulled together into an overall structure. In response, the personal sense of time is introspective, digging deep inside the human consciousness and emotions, which may be a way of resisting these social conventions and their mechanical approach to temporality. Fragments of events are brought together through consciousness, memory and identity, offering a temporal connectivity as an alternative to the instrumental grid of time. Temporal frameworks, quantitative and qualitative, help create social institutions and personal narratives about the events that have happened, are happening now and are going to happen in the future. Collective memory and identity are public discourses that can bind the temporal fragments together, but they are subject to the power relations that need to be scrutinized and made accountable.

The identity of cities can be studied at the interface of the relations of similarity and difference: how a place is similar to, and different from, others. These relations are articulated through narratives which connect disparate pieces and integrate them into a unified and apparently coherent whole. Narratives, however, are themselves diverse, told by different people, situated in different parts of the society and towards different ends. The process through which a narrative emerges, through which the identity of place is articulated, is subject to tensions and power struggles, resulting in a diversity of trajectories for the future of a place. These narratives of identity both reflect the political structures and cultural preferences of a society, as well as the efforts of individuals and groups to introduce new stories and more complex identities. The only way a multifaceted story can be heard is through dynamic multiplicity: listening to many voices over time, but always open to questions. The higher frequency of temporary events may have undermined these narratives, turning them into ever-changing stories. The interface between a rapid movement of temporality and the stabling effects of narratives may become a point of instability itself. Can such stability be found in the natural environment and the material world?

5

Nature, Time and Anxiety

So far, we have seen how events are linked together through a mechanical grid and social institutions, as well as intuitions and personal experiences, and how both are affected by temporary events and temporal acceleration. In this chapter, the focus is on the linkages made to the natural environment. The chapter is organized in six parts. It first introduces the paradoxical approaches to nature in the modern period, and the way nature has been understood within the human body and in the wider natural world, both showing a dichotomous and ambiguous relationship. The natural world within the human body has been split into a mind–body distinction, while the natural world around us has turned from being a subject of conquest to one of concern. The state of nature as a state of apparent originality refers to a nostalgic memory of the time that humans lived in apparent harmony with the natural world, while the absence of this harmony and the fragility of the natural world is vividly experienced today. The result is a sense of contingency and anxiety about the future, which is exacerbated by temporal acceleration.

The paradoxes of nature

The natural world has been a paradox for the modern society: thought to be at once orderly and unruly, at once ingrained in us and separate from us, and at once a realm of predictability and contingency. On the one hand, it has been considered to be a highly ordered system, with hidden and universal laws which need to be discovered by science. On the other hand, the natural world has been conceptualized as wild, with powerful and unpredictable forces that need to be tamed and conquered by science and technology, and understood and represented by the arts. An associated paradox has been the place of humans in this natural world: standing outside this world with the aim of conquering it, while being one of its integral parts. The paradox acknowledges that we share many of our features with other animals and life forms, while imagining and conceptualizing the human species as occupying a place well above the rest. It envisages a dualism between a body that we share with the natural world and a mind that stands above it. At once highly ordered and wild, ruled by universal laws and unpredictable forces, including humans and subordinate to them, the natural world has been understood and approached in paradoxical ways.

This paradoxical approach is also visible in the different meanings that are associated with the word 'nature'. According to Raymond Williams (1985:219), 'Nature is probably the most complex word in the language'. Some have used it to refer to unchanging phenomena and fixed identities, while others have even questioned the existence of such a thing as nature, arguing that it is merely a social construction. The *Oxford English Dictionary* provides two distinctive meanings for the word. On the one hand, it refers to 'the phenomena of the physical world collectively, including plants, animals, the landscape, and other features and products of the earth, as opposed to humans or human creations'. The ambiguity of this meaning lies in its reference to the 'physical world' as a whole, which would inevitably include the humans, while at the same time being distinctive from them. It generates a distinctive 'other' which is nevertheless intertwined at all times with human affairs. On the other hand, the word refers to 'the basic or inherent features, character, or qualities of something'. This second meaning of the word refers to something deep inside that is not immediately visible and that needs to be discovered. It assumes some essential features that lie at the heart of something's identity. The two meanings, therefore, expand horizontally and vertically, to cover the entire world as well as what lies beneath it. Both meanings, meanwhile, have an ambiguous relationship to the place of humans. In many discourses, the word 'nature' is used in a way that may refer both to surface and depth, both the physical world as a whole and the inherent features of its constituent elements, both the multiplicity and singularity of phenomena, and both the contingency and fixity of these phenomena.

The balance between contingency and certainty, however, is always shifting. In some periods, cultures and circumstances, the sense of confidence grows, followed by a strong trust in the universal rules, orderly world and human ability to make sense of both the multiplicity and singularity of the phenomena, and to control them at will. When the confidence is shaken, however, the unpredictability, unruliness and contingency of the world are rediscovered, while doubt about the human abilities grows. The history of civilizations may show these rises and falls of confidence, this shifting balance between certainty and anxiety. The extent of anxiety about the natural world, however, has never been as deep as the current period of environmental crisis. The comparable accounts about a time in which the entire world was endangered may have been the ancient Mesopotamian epic of Gilgamesh and the biblical story of Noah, recounting the tale of a flood that had covered the world, threatening life on earth; but in both stories disaster had been averted by a boat carrying representatives of all species. While in these stories only a chosen few could survive the flood, no such confidence and support may be available today, as the scale and scope of the risk to life on earth has been far more substantial, from the threat of inundation of large cities and entire countries to droughts and storms and the extinction of species.

The paradoxical approaches to the natural world also include a balance of change and permanence. The natural world is in continual change, but its overall continuity and durability are a source of psychological security and permanence for the human species. At once, therefore, it is a process of change and a framework for stability. The scale and speed of change in the natural world appear to be slow and rhythmical, and the continual reproduction of this material world gives it the appearance of continuity and stability, especially in the context of cosmological and geological sense of time. However, when change in the natural world seems to be faster and more unpredictable, or predictable in ways that are potentially dangerous to the conditions of life on earth, the sense of permanence is disrupted; the aspect of change takes over, undermining the aspect of durability and permanence. Therefore, when this framework of stability seems to be jeopardized the sense of anxiety rises. Rather than a permanent environment, we realize that we are living in a temporary one, exposed to many risks that we have unwittingly caused or magnified. At first glance, temporary events might seem to be at odds with the natural world, about which a sense of permanence is somehow embedded in the human psyche. But when the natural world is seen as a temporary one itself, the parallels become more obvious. Temporariness therefore describes the fragility of life on earth, rediscovering the vulnerability of everything on earth to the natural events, from cities to forests and seas.

There are two ways in which permanence is conceptualized in nature: the nature within humans and the natural world around us. However, with the discovery of evolution and the decentring of the subject, the permanence of the nature within evaporates, and with the environmental crisis, the natural world is in danger of decline. Both of these forms of contingency create a sense of vulnerability and anxiety towards future (Heidegger), which is reflected in the temporariness of what we do, as the long-term prospects seem to recede.

The nature within: From unity to multiplicity

The interest in the way nature has been reflected within the humans has focused on the body and mind, sometimes privileging one and at other times the other. During the renaissance, the human body became the source of inspiration for the architects, who looked for harmony and beauty, and the human mind for the philosophers, who looked for certainty and proof. Both of these sources of a permanent basis for thought and action, however, have now shown to be vulnerable.

In the Renaissance, when humanism replaces medieval religiosity, a return to Greek and Roman ideas places nature, and in particular the human body, at the centre of the world. Nature is well ordered and harmonious, and the task of architecture is to learn and replicate this natural order. Geometrical shapes are the expression of this order and harmony, and the human body is the origin of its proportions and measures. Human body is the finest expression of nature's proportions, and geometry is the way humans capture and reconstruct the natural order.

Filarete, the designer of the first utopian city of the Renaissance, wrote his *Treatise on Architecture* between 1461 and 1464, describing in detail the principles and the design of the ideal city of Sforzinda, named after the Duke of Milan (Madanipour, 2016). Its star shape was the result of 'two squares, one atop the other without the angles touching' (Filarete, 1965:25). He explicitly locates his commitment to geometrical perfection in the harmonies and proportions that are found in human body and in nature. He starts his treatise by stating that all the 'proportions, qualities, measure, and their origin... derive from the figure and form of man' (Filarete, 1965:5). Human body, in turn, is proportioned on the basis of the size of a human head: 'the head is the most noble and most beautiful member' (Filarete, 1965:8). All parts of the body are multiples of the head, and this harmonious proportionality gives rise to perfect geometrical shapes: 'if the arms are opened and the hands extended, [the man] will be nine heads in either direction' (Filarete, 1965:8). With the navel at its centre, a man may be circumscribed in a circle centred on the navel; this is where the circle is derived.

For Flireate, the origins of architecture lie in nature, as articulated in the figure and proportions of human body (Figure 5.1). The three ancient architectural orders, Doric, Corinthian and Ionic, reflected three sizes of a body: large (nine heads, the size of the first and the most beautiful human Adam), medium (eight heads) and small (seven heads). Commonly used measures are also based on the parts of the human body, such as hands and arms, all proportioned with the head. Buildings are also understood to be analogous to human beings: 'the building is truly a living man' (Filarete, 1965:15). This humanism is reflected in much of the art of the Renaissance, in painting, sculpture and architecture, as exemplified by Leonardo da Vinci, Ghiberti and Alberti. Leon Battista Alberti, who presented his own treatise on architecture to Pope Nicholas V in 1452, a decade before Filarete, also compares the building to human body, whose proportions were harmonious and needed to be replicated. Like in music, harmony was the keyword, and it

FIGURE 5.1 *Filarete, the designer of the first ideal city of Renaissance and of this castle gate, drew inspiration from the natural world, but was also aware of the possible implications of imposing a utopian geometry on it (Milan, Italy).*

was therefore important to avoid buildings that would 'appear like a monster with uneven shoulders and side'. While variety was pleasant, it could cause discord and difference and thereby become 'extremely disagreeable' (Alberti, 1988:24).

With the discovery of the laws of perspective and the emerging humanist attitudes, buildings were now designed to have a central point, reflecting the significance of centrality in this anthropomorphic world. Central planning found its boldest expression in town planning, such as Alberti's plan for Rome, which proposed an obelisk in the middle of one of plazas in front of St Peter's, and in Filarete's placing a high tower in the middle of his city. According to Pevsner (1963), this central planning, which was a Roman type of building, was revived as the prime manifestation of humanism and was the key to the Renaissance and Baroque architecture.

> For a central plan is not an other-worldly, but a this-worldly conception. The prime function of the medieval church had been to lead the faithful to the altar. In a completely centralized building no such movement is possible. The building has its full effect only when it is looked at from the one focal point. There the spectator must stand and, by standing there, he becomes himself 'the measure of all things'. Thus the religious meaning of the church is replaced by a human one. Man is in the church no longer pressing forward to reach a transcendental goal, but enjoying the beauty that surrounds him and the glorious sensation of being the centre of this beauty. (Pevsner, 1963:182)

Central planning was also expressed in the idea of a single designer for the city and its rules, anticipating the rise of absolute monarchies. Machiavelli believed in the importance of a single source of legal and political design: 'as a general rule: seldom or never is any republic or kingdom organized well … except when organized by one man' (quoted in Skinner, 1981:63). In a similar vein, Descartes argued for a single designer for the city as the source of its order and harmony.

> So it is that one sees that buildings undertaken and completed by a single architect are usually more beautiful and better ordered than those that several architects have tried to put into shape, making use of old walls which were built for other purposes. So it is that these old cities which originally were only villages, have become, through the passage of time, great towns, are usually so badly proportioned in comparison with those orderly towns which an engineer designs at will on some plain that, although the buildings, taken separately, often display as much art as those of the planned towns or even more, nevertheless, seeing how they are placed, with a big one here, a small one there, and how they cause the streets to bend and to be at different levels, one has the impression that they are more the product of chance than of a human will operating according to reason. (Descartes, 1968:35)

Centrality of the body and political institutions were linked with the centrality of the mind. Descartes is credited to have shifted the centre of gravity in philosophy to the human mind, thereby laying the cornerstone of modern philosophy. He was looking for certainty for his beliefs, and he found it in his own intuitions. To find a solution to the problem of doubt about the sources of knowledge, he started by arguing that beliefs were based on custom and example, and that our senses could be misleading. But what was not doubtful was that there was an internal source who was doubting. Even if everything was an illusion, it was clear that 'I who thought thus must be something ... I think, therefore I am' (Descartes, 1968:53). With this shift of focus from the social and metaphysical world to the world inside the human mind, he could find a secure basis on which to develop a system of beliefs. According to these views that had evolved over several centuries to develop the idea of an autonomous individual self, the nature within us, both in terms of the human body and mind, was the source of harmony, power and belief. This integrated centre of gravity, however, was soon challenged, decentred into a vulnerable bundle of desires and dreams.

A turning point was the argument by David Hume in the eighteenth century about the primacy of passions and desires. He questioned the prevalence of reason in human actions: 'Reason is, and ought only to be the slave of the passions, and can never pretend to any other office than to serve and obey them' (Hume, 1985:462). Passion was 'an original existence', and it was the primary motive in human action, as in fact, 'Nothing can oppose or retard the impulse of passion, but a contrary impulse' (Hume, 1985:462). Reason alone, therefore, did not occupy the driving seat of human thoughts and actions, as its role was limited to the discovery of the relations between objects and the distinction between truth and falsehood. As he wrote, 'Since a passion can never, in any sense, be called unreasonable, but when founded on a false supposition, or when it chooses means insufficient for the designed end, 'tis impossible, that reason and passion can ever oppose each other, or dispute for the government of the will and action' (Hume, 1985:464). The implications of such a shift in thinking have been long-lasting and profound, as it has led to a complete change of attitude towards the nature that lies within human beings.

A later development in the nineteenth century that transformed the concept of human being was Darwin's theory of evolution of species, which showed how human beings were an integral part of a process of change shared by all other life forms and inanimate objects. It was no longer possible to separate the human species to have a privileged position, standing above and apart from the rest of the natural world. The nature within had been transformed to become fully in line with the nature without, as the evolution of species worked in its process of adaptation to the environment.

The concept of the nature within was also transformed with changing cultural and philosophical outlooks, which investigated the concepts of mind, body and identity. An essentialist approach that would search for a permanent and unchanging nature in human beings was challenged by the argument that such an essence does not exist prior to existence. The existentialists, such as Kierkegaard (2014), Heidegger (1962) and Sartre (2003), have argued that human existence unfolds with time, rather than being predetermined, and that it is up to humans to determine what shape their life will take. Psychoanalysts referred to an unknown world inside the human psyche that would be driven by desire and at odds with social norms and practices (Freud, 1985). This idea was in sharp contrast to the Cartesian concept of self which was reliable and unchanging (Descartes, 1968). The human self was now made of many parts, without a stable core, each time taking a new form and content, driven by repetition of desires in different forms and guises (Smith and Somershall, 2012).

For Descartes, mind and body were completely separate entities: in what is called Cartesian dualism (Cottingham, 1992a), he argued that the mind (or soul) is non-physical and is distinct from the body or other material objects: '... this "I", that is to say, the mind, by which I am what I am, is entirely distinct from the body' (Descartes, 1968:54). The shift from body to mind had demonstrated a shift in attitudes towards the place of humans in the natural world. The value of the body, and with it the value of the material world of nature, was undermined in favour of the intellectual powers of the mind. Humans were associated with their rationality and their ability to control their natural impulses. Such dualism is now widely rejected in a more integrated view of the mind and body (Cottingham, 1992b; Searle, 1999; Žižek, 1999; Dennett, 2013). The influence of the body on mental states is acknowledged by psychoanalysts (Freud, 1985). Neuroscientists have also argued for the interaction between the body and the brain, and against the idea that our mind is entirely working within the brain without any interface with the rest of the body (Greenfield, 2000; Bennett et al., 2003).

The self was ultimately shaped by social norms and practices (Hegel, 1967; Taylor, 1989; Bourdieu, 2000), rather than an innate nature that would determine its manifestation. If once the world was taken to be a manifestation of permanent Ideas (Plato, 1993), now it was taken to be continually changing, never set on a permanent path or revealing a permanent core. Human beings are a part of an ever-changing natural and social world, and their biology, character and identity always change alongside the changing world around them. The problem of identity is a long-standing problem in philosophy: the question has been whether with the passage of time, a person remains the same or becomes a different person. If the continuity of self is open to question, the problem of identity becomes more acute, as it becomes difficult to show how a person remains the same if there is no single core but it is made of many parts, and its sense of time is one of a multiplicity, as discussed in Chapter 4.

Deep and unchanging truths about the nature of the self, therefore, were not to be found. Previous generations had argued that all we could find about the world was the appearances (Kant, 1993). What mattered was to focus on these appearances as they are reflected in our mind (Husserl, 1991). This would prepare the ground for removing the idea of a permanent nature for things, as the only way we have access to the world is through our ever-changing sense and perceptions. A world of phenomena would be a continually changing world, and if there are any permanent features, we would not have any way of finding them; we only have our changing senses and perceptions. To overcome this limitation, and finding some solid foundations, we may produce names and concepts, so that they establish a stable layer of representation in relation to a changing reality. But if these representations are open to critique and revision, rather than eternal truths, then the notion of a permanent nature in the self, or our representations of the self and the world, may all evaporate. The disappearance of such a solid ground may engender a sense of emancipation, but also a feeling of vulnerability and anxiety.

Despite these critiques, the legacies of humanist and rationalist thinking have continued in many guises, most notably in the modernist movement since the twentieth century. The references to the human body and its proportions as a basis for architecture, the application of geometry to architecture and city design and the possibility of a rationalist reorganization of space are all present in the work of Le Corbusier (1986; 1987). This time, however, it was not drawing on nature as a source of inspiration and imitation, as Renaissance humanists had done, but mobilizing efforts to conquer and transform it, in line with the later rationalists.

Nature without: From conquest to concern

In parallel with the transition in thinking about the nature within human bodies, a transition took place in the relationship between human society and the natural world, in other words, the nature without. From a desire for the conquest of nature, the humanity has moved to a situation of concern for the natural world, as its vulnerabilities and the impact of human action on this world have become manifest. The permanence of the natural world, which was seen as a counterpoint to the ephemerality of the human world, now seems at the point of receding and evaporating. The relationship between the human species and the natural environment has always combined elements of struggle and submission, evolving from harmony to battle and ultimately to anxiety.

In addition to being inspired by the nature within the human body, Filarete's new city had ambiguous relationships with the natural environment in which it was to be located, which was now due to be transformed by the construction of a utopian city. Filarete (1965) describes an imaginary short journey into a rural idyll which he considers to be the best location for his new city. The site of the new city was in a very pleasant valley, with its fertile land, plentiful water supplied by the river and well protected from undesirable winds by the surrounding mountains. Its woods were teeming with wild life and its lands produced the best agricultural produce. Filarete, however, is well aware of the possible negative impact of the new development. An imaginary gentleman host welcomes him to the valley, feeds him in his house and shows him around the area. The host, however, becomes worried about the new city's implications for the natural environment: 'If any city is built here this wood will be cut down' (Filarete, 1965:25). Filarete reassures his host that this wood would not be touched and trees from other forests will be used in the construction of the city, transported to the site via the river.

The anxiety of the farmer and the reassurance of the city builder show an age-old tension between urban development and the natural environment. It also shows a dichotomous attitude to nature that is still with us today – on the one hand praising it for its beauty and harmony and on the other hand transforming it through urban development, thereby jeopardizing the health of the natural environment and generating anxiety about its future. The ambiguous and dichotomous attitude which is visible in this early Renaissance example is one that has magnified to unprecedented proportions, creating anxieties about the survival of many species and even life as a whole. The roots of our current concerns for the natural world go back to the rise of this Renaissance confidence in human abilities in understanding and conquering nature. As Francis Bacon announced, human beings were 'the servant and interpreter of Nature', which they could do so only by observation, rather than 'all those specious meditations, speculations, and glosses in which men indulge' (Bacon, 1995:39). With growing confidence, Descartes displayed the preference for dominance over nature, endeavouring to 'make ourselves, as it were, masters and possessors of nature' (Descartes, 1968:78).

The implications of change for the natural environment, however, were not fully recognized before the nineteenth-century expansion of urban areas that followed the emergence of industrial capitalism in Europe (Figure 5.2). Our current approaches to the natural world are the most recent phase in a long-standing dichotomy between the Enlightenment and the Romantic movements that emerged at the dawn of the modern age. For the eighteenth-century Enlightenment, and its predecessors in Renaissance, nature was an orderly phenomenon with universal laws that could be discovered by science (Hollis, 2002) and conquered by technology. For the nineteenth-century

FIGURE 5.2 *The romantic response to the industrial culture has been a nostalgia for the natural world (Tampere, Finland).*

romantics, nature was the realm of feelings, originality, spontaneity and freedom, a contrast to the artificial and sterile orders of rationalism. For the romantics, however, nature was far from unitary or simple; it was complex and diverse. As Quinton (2005) wrote:

> The Romantic favours the concrete over the abstract, variety over uniformity, the infinite over the finite, nature over culture, convention, and artifice, the organic over the mechanical, freedom over constraint, rules, and limitations. In human terms it prefers the unique individual to the average man, the free creative genius to the prudent man of good sense, the particular community or nation to humanity at large. Mentally the Romantic prefers feeling to thought, more specifically, emotion to calculation, imagination to literal common-sense, intuition to intellect.

The interplay of these two contrasting approaches to nature has created and shaped the way nature is understood and treated up to this day.

The motto of the Enlightenment, as proclaimed by Immanuel Kant (1995:1), was 'Have courage to use your own reason'. It was by this reason that universal scientific and ethical principles could be found and applied. As

Leibniz had argued in his key principle, everything has a reason (Heidegger, 1996). The modern philosophy and science was searching for this reason, which frequently was preferably a single reason that would explain everything. Isaac Newton called his principles of gravity the law of nature, one which united the terrestrial and celestial laws, hitherto treated as separate realms, into a single formula. According to Isaac Newton (1995:45), 'Nature is pleased with simplicity', which he thought could be expressed in mathematical principles. The law of gravity was the unifying principle that could explain the underlying order of the universe. Long before Newtown, pre-Socratic philosophers in Greece had looked for a single principle that would explain the universe as a whole. It was made of fire, water or change. The idea of a unified principle is also evident in monotheistic religions that have argued for a single cause to the world order. After Newton, many scientists have looked for a unitary principle, a theory of everything, which would explain the processes of the natural world in a single formula. Einstein famously spent many years in search of such a unifying principle. The belief in simplicity, orderliness and unity of the natural world offered the possibility of certainty and predictability. These principles, however, have never been found, as the laws of nature only apply to some situations and fields, rather than every possible situation and at all times.

In the divide between the classical and romantic traditions, temporary events may be interpreted to have completely different meanings and implications. In the classical tradition, which the Renaissance and the Enlightenment embraced and revived, nature is the course of harmony and order. Temporary events would undermine this orderliness, and while they may be unavoidable in certain circumstances, they cannot become the norm. The romantic tradition, which shares many features with the medieval sentiments, looks at such ruptures with open arms, as they could be a possible path to freedom and the emergence of new possibilities for the future. Depending on the perspective, a rupture could be interpreted as an inconvenient digression or a path to emancipation.

Nature as an original state

For most of its life on earth, the human species had lived in harmony with the natural environment, living with what was immediately available in the surrounding areas. For 2.4 million years, the Homo species was a forager, living by hunting, fishing and gathering wild plants. As the environmental resources were limited, they lived in small bands that continuously moved in search of food (Bouquet-Appel, 2011). Areas with rich resources enabled some groups to delineate flexible territories within which they could hunt wild animals and gather food. As the availability of food varied in different seasons and different parts of land, the size of this territory needed to be large enough to support a family group and to allow for the replenishment of the used resources for future takings. Their way of life was well integrated into the natural environment, and like all of its other elements, it was at once precarious and contingent while being continuous and relatively well-established. Living for millions of years under these conditions has formed the image of an 'original' state for humanity, shaping its earliest memories and some of its biological and psychological features. Evolutionary psychologists believe that this long formative period of foraging has left its marks on many of the basic instincts and patterns of behaviour in modern humans (Figure 5.3).

The relationship with nature was shaped by small interactions within natural limits and affordance, rather than transformation and conquest. It continued after the emergence of Homo sapiens, but was radically transformed around 12 millennia ago. The transition from foraging to farming had a considerable impact on human relations with the environment, turning it from living within what the natural environment offered to support a small band of hunter-gatherers to living in settled communities that would transform the land around them, thereby producing food beyond their immediate needs. Since then, farmers have transformed the natural environment beyond recognition, through deforestation, irrigation and cultivation (Figure 5.4). In farming,

FIGURE 5.3 *For millions of years, the natural environment and the place of humans in it seemed to be timeless (Johannesburg, South Africa).*

FIGURE 5.4 *For the past 12 millennia, farmers have transformed the natural environment beyond recognition (Northumberland, UK).*

however, we were still constrained by the limits of the environment, water, land and location, which all had an impact on the lives of farmers, hence the continuous concern for rain or protection from the extremes of weather conditions.

These past ways of life as foragers and farmers have left their deep marks on human psyche and experience. The twelve millennia of agricultural period is much shorter than the foraging period, but also closer to our current experience, forming the basis of many of humanity's beliefs, social institutions, philosophical concepts, means of communication and expression. The urban explosion of the contemporary period has produced its own patterns of life, but it is also substantially indebted to the previous periods of human history. In some parts of the world, life as industrial workers has now been added to these traces of the past, joining the memories of foragers and farmers. The instincts, ideals and memories that were developed in previous epochs, however, are used in completely different circumstances, leading to challenges and frustrations at their mismatch with the circumstances of living in the continually shifting urban environments of today.

The nineteenth-century revolutionaries and romantics went back to this original state to discover what it means to be human. The romantics glorified this early life that was in harmony with nature, and the social revolutionaries praised the idea of small communes with egalitarian habits. These early forms of life, or the state of nature as some early modern thinkers called them, however, have been interpreted in different ways: as a time of savagery and darkness or a period of innocence, peace and equality. For Hobbes, the possibility of equality in the state of nature led to competition and war, whereby life would be 'solitary, poor, nasty, brutish, and short', only to be avoided by submission to an omnipotent sovereign (Hobbes, 1985:186). For Rousseau, who has been considered to be an inspiration for romantics and revolutionaries, the state of nature was a state of happiness and freedom, while living in society was a state of slavery and loss of freedom: 'Man is born free, and he is everywhere in chains' (Rousseau, 1968:49). However, living in civil society offered far greater advantages in return for the surrender of some liberties, turning the human being from 'a stupid, limited animal' to 'a creature of intelligence and a man' (Rousseau, 1968:64–5).

It was in the context of disconnection from nature and this ambiguous stance towards it that the romantics escaped from the city into the countryside (Figure 5.5). The early Romantic poets like Wordsworth and Coleridge were fascinated by the natural landscape, taking refuge in the English Lake District,

FIGURE 5.5 *The romantic attitude advocates a return to the natural world and a simpler way of life (Lake Como, Italy).*

where they could be far from the busy life of the emerging industrial cities. Although a return to the countryside represented selecting a simpler lifestyle, and a return to an original state of nature, it was not an attempt to simplify nature. Indeed, the complexity and diversity of the natural world was the source of aesthetic pleasure, as exemplified by the picturesque movement. The arts no longer aimed at imitating human action, and a radical departure from the classical tradition took place (Thacker, 1983), giving its place to the art of sublime that portrayed the wilderness, from the mountains and coasts to ruins and fields (Hawes, 1982). The wilderness was no longer a dark and uncivilized place, but a place of purity and originality and an escape from the city, as desired by Henry David Thoreau: 'Let me live where I will, on this side is the city, on that side the wilderness, and I am ever leaving the city more and more, and withdrawing into the wilderness' (quoted in McKusick, 2000:2). The modern environmental movement draws heavily on this romantic tradition, from Rousseau to Coleridge, Wordsworth and Blake. According to the editor of an anthology on green studies, 'Sometimes we may have the feeling that we are only just catching up with Wordsworth' (Coupe, 2000:6).

For these writers, poets and painters, however, nature was still a symbol of permanence, a place of security and a welcoming bosom to escape into. John Clare, the English poet of the countryside who lived in the first half of the nineteenth century, wrote about the eternity of nature and the ephemerality of the modern industrial urbanism (Clare, 1984). The titles of a number of his poems include the word 'eternity' as a feature of nature, such as 'Eternity of Nature', 'Song's Eternity' and 'Invitation to Eternity'. In a poem entitled 'Eternity of Nature', he wrote about the continuity of life as it ran through the woods, fields and brooks; their change was not a sign of mortality but of life, which would continually revive and rejuvenate. In the poem entitled 'Song's Eternity', he wrote about how 'Crowds and cities pass away – like a day', and how books die, whereas the music of creation that is sung in nature is an eternal one. By our time, however, this sense of security and purity seems to be ever out of reach in a planet that is considerably changed by human action. It is this sense of eternity that is deeply jeopardized by the current concerns about the planet and its future; what appeared to be permanent is now felt to be ephemeral.

During the past two centuries, many attempts have been made to protect the countryside from urban encroachment and to build bridges between society and nature. Building bridges with nature included bringing countryside elements into the city, as reflected in tree-lined boulevards and parks, and increasingly new forms of greenery on walls, roofs and anywhere that could be called a green asset as part of a green infrastructure. From public parks, boulevards and private gardens to temporary urban beaches, the desire to restore the broken links between the urban and the natural worlds has been evident for centuries (Figure 5.6). The romantic desire for living in

FIGURE 5.6 *From the nineteenth-century public parks and boulevards to the twenty-first-century temporary beaches, the natural world has been brought into the city to restore the disconnected relationship (Newcastle, UK).*

the countryside was indeed the vanguard of a process of suburbanization, whereby city dwellers escape from the city but do not go far, looking for an in-between condition that would include access to both town and countryside. The countryside, even though highly managed and manufactured, stood for the idea of an authentic nature free from human intervention. A small suburban garden was all they needed to feel in touch with the delights of nature. Garden cities, new towns and other forms of suburban development have all shown attempts to offer this bridge into the natural world. Ironically, however, these developments have enlarged the urban footprint, adding to the magnitude of the climate crisis.

From the end of the eighteenth century, in the face of the emerging modernity, which reshaped the society and unsettled the old beliefs and practices, the natural environment became a refuge for those who were searching for certainty and stability. The current environmental crisis, however, shows that even the continuity and permanence of this source of certainty is no longer guaranteed, as the natural environment is threatened with major changes. While it has long been understood that the natural world is continually changing, this change has been placed in the context of a stable notion of the natural order. Now even those stable points of reference in the natural world are being shaken, and with them the trust in their permanence. The anxiety about the changing society has now been extended to a changing nature, magnifying and spreading the sense of ephemerality. Cultural ephemerality reflects this sense of insecurity which is increasingly felt in both the social and the natural worlds.

Fragile nature

The increasingly fragile balance of forces on the planet earth, which sustains human life, has vividly reminded us of our fragility as a species (Figure 5.7). According to the Intergovernmental Panel on Climate Change, as a result of the recent anthropogenic emissions of greenhouse gases, which are the highest in history, the earth's climate has changed at unprecedented levels. 'Warming of the climate system is unequivocal, and since the 1950s, many of the observed changes are unprecedented over decades to millennia. The atmosphere and ocean have warmed, the amounts of snow and ice have

FIGURE 5.7 *Climate change and mismanagement have dried the river, turning the historic bridge into a stand-alone building and taking away an integral part of the city's identity and the citizens' quality of life (Isfahan, Iran).*

diminished, and sea level has risen' (IPCC, 2014:40). The impacts of climate change have been observed in all parts of the world in physical systems (glaciers, snow, ice and/or permafrost; rivers, lakes, floods and/or drought; coastal erosion and/or sea level effects), in biological systems (terrestrial ecosystems, wildfire, marine ecosystems) and in human and managed systems (food production, livelihoods, health and/or economy) (IPCC, 2014:50). This would increase vulnerability and exposure to the risk and harm caused by these changes, which are magnified in the case of disadvantaged and marginalized populations, who may additionally suffer from some of the mitigation and adaptation responses to climate change. These hazards would directly affect the lives of the poor, whose livelihoods would suffer from the fall in crop yields and destruction of homes, or indirectly through higher food prices and lower food security (IPCC, 2014:54).

An example is the impact of the rising sea levels. Over the past century, global warming has melted land and sea ice, from icebergs to mountain glaciers and ice caps. A complete meltdown of the world's two major ice sheets, Greenland and Antarctica, would raise the sea levels by 75 metres, enough to submerge a large part of the human habitat (Graham, 1999). The rising sea levels have already threatened the survival of some islands. As the prime minister of the small island nation of Tuvalu warned the United Nations' General Assembly in 2003, 'We live in constant fear of the adverse impacts of climate change. For a coral atoll nation, sea level rise and more severe weather events loom as a growing threat to our entire population. The threat is real and serious' (Tuvalu Islands, 2010). Larger nations are similarly vulnerable; one of the most vulnerable is Bangladesh which, with its more than 150 million populations, could lose 17 per cent of its land and 30 per cent of its food production by 2050, putting pressure on its growing population to squeeze into a smaller country vulnerable to river floods and sea level rise. More than half of the population are already affected by salinity and millions of people in northern Bangladesh are threatened by riverbank erosion and severe droughts (Ibne Mahmood, 2012).

Existential threat is also present at the heart of the rich nations, as exemplified by Katrina and Sandy hurricanes in the United States. Hurricane Sandy, which hit New York in 2012, killed 159 people, damaged or destroyed at least 650,000 homes and 250,500 insured vehicles, altogether causing $65 billion in damages (Rice and Dastagir, 2013). Sandy showed the extent of New York City's vulnerability to climatic disasters. London's Thames Barrier spans 520 metres across the river Thames near Woolwich, protecting 125 square kilometres of central London from flooding caused by tidal surges. Since its start of operations in 1982, the Thames Barrier has been used 175 times against tidal and river floods, of which more than a third has happened in the last five years, indicating a rise in these incidents (Environment Agency, 2015). Large parts of London and the Thames Estuary, including 500,000 homes, large parts of its underground system and its major institutions such as the Houses of Parliament and the government district of Whitehall, its financial centres such as the Docklands and its Port, are within the natural floodplain of Thames, vulnerable to the tidal surges caused by rising sea levels, which requires new planned responses for the future (Environment Agency, 2012).

Witnessing the disappearance of ice sheets, of wildlife and the visible impact of climate change on human life has caused a new, more vulnerable sense of time. The two world wars, and particularly the threat of nuclear winter during the Cold War, had created an inherent sense of vulnerability, whereby the entire human species could disappear in a moment of human madness. The response was pressure for disarmament, which could in theory be achieved within a short period of time. But now the threat of environmental annihilation requires a much harder effort, which does not seem to be forthcoming. The immediacy of threat is replaced by a long-term existential threat, in which the future generations will face challenges inherited from the past. The feeling of unease grows, frustrated by the denial of climate change or of human influence on it, or by the lack of coordinated action to confront it. As the threat is global, the response needs to be equally coordinated at the global level, hence the immense problems that need to be confronted if such a global response is to be mobilized (Rees, 2014). The contingency of life, and in particular human life, and the vulnerability of the large concentrations of people in cities to such threats, undermine the trust in a predictable and safe future, especially for the rich nations who are used to higher levels of safety and predictability.

To confront this anxiety, various terms have been used, ranging from sustainability to resilience. Whereas sustainability was formulated as the response to the environmental crisis in a more optimistic and positive way, resilience signifies a more nervous reaction. In the discourses of sustainability, the emphasis was on a careful use of resources, so that the needs of the future generations be also maintained. As famously defined by the Brundtland report, 'sustainable development is development that meets the needs of the present without compromising the ability of future generations to meet their own needs' (Bruntland, 1987). It is a call for intergenerational equality, for the guardianship of the earth's dwindling resources and the potential negative impact of our current trends on the future. Now, however, the term 'resilience' seems to have become commonplace, indicating the pressure to be ready for the imminent disaster and to be prepared to 'bounce back' from what seems to have already happened. It is no longer a situation of calm contemplation, but a rescue effort for returning to normalcy. The term 'resilience' seems to have combined the threats of economic crisis, terrorism and climate change under a single umbrella. It is, therefore, an indication of a heightened feeling of anxiety and unease, and the need to develop the ability to stand up after falling down, rather than trying to avoid such a fall.

Temporality, contingency and anxiety

Anxiety about the future, which is always unknown and unknowable, is a fundamental human condition. Kierkegaard (2014) developed the notion of anxiety, which was already present in the early nineteenth-century romanticism, as a centrepiece of his ideas. He used it to develop the notion of a single individual, which he thought to be his primary contribution, as capable of reflecting the manner of its existence and its place in the world. For him, anxiety could be a productive force, with the possibility of leading to spiritual fulfilment. 'Anxiety', Kierkegaard (2014:xviii) wrote, 'is in fact a desire for what one fears'. Heidegger, following Kierkegaard but without his theological intentions, identifies anxiety as a basic state of mind.

Heidegger makes a distinction between fear and anxiety: fear is the result of encountering something in the world, but anxiety is caused by the unknown. It is just the result of being in the world. As such, Heidegger (1962:231) argues, 'That in the face of which one is anxious is completely indefinite', it is 'characterized by the fact that what threatens is nowhere'. We feel anxious but are not sure about what it is about; in other words, 'It is nothing and nowhere', which suggests that 'the world as such is that in the face of which one has anxiety' (Heidegger, 1962:231). Anxiety is a basic state of mind, which manifests *Dasein*'s potential to be free to choose and to be authentic. As Heidegger (1962:38) interprets *Dasein* as temporality, a direct link is made between temporality and anxiety: the basic state of mind is anxiety about being in the world, and as being is inherently temporal, it is anxiety about an unknown future that continuously unfolds.

By calling anxiety a basic state of mind, Heidegger is proposing a universal condition for all human beings. This global anxiety, however, is not the same as anxiety about specific events. The differences of temperaments and circumstances would also complicate this analysis further. Anxiety as a mood and a state of mind is manifested differently and it is possible to observe the different levels of anxiety that rise and fall according to by whom and under what conditions it is experienced or even not felt at all. In the situations that vulnerability and instability are increased, the sense of anxiety would also rise, and the situations of calm and stability reduce or even remove the sense of anxiety. The sense of anxiety would also depend on the temperament of individuals, and as such would be different for those who are highly sensitive to real or imagined changes of circumstance and the consequent vulnerabilities. While Heidegger's analysis of metaphysics rests on the sense of anxiety as a basic state of mind, we can therefore see how in the realm of experience this anxiety ebbs and flows and it may not be present at all times and for all people. When the universality of anxiety confronts the realm of difference, therefore, the possibility of universality diminishes.

Anxiety about the unknown future is a response to the contingency of our conditions. The sense of anxiety reveals the trembling anticipation of vulnerability and disorder, engendering a series of phobias towards the unknown. The response may be a magnified desire for order and stability. This is evident in the discourse of resilience, which emphasizes the need for security and therefore tightening the laws and strengthening the forces of control and order. Rather than temporality as the cause of anxiety per se, we might consider contingency as the condition which induces the sense of vulnerability and anxiety. Its presence may generate a mood of ambiguity and a generalized sense of unease about the future, or it may lead to a clear state of mind in which contingency is confronted with a plan of action. The absence of contingency, or at least the awareness of a state of contingency, meanwhile, may lead to a state of calm and confidence, rather than anxiety and malaise. The emphasis on contingency would lead us to the analysis of the material conditions in which contingency is generated and confronted. We may broaden the psychological analysis of moods and states of mind to the social and historical circumstances in which contingency is heightened or managed. While the periods of prosperity had engendered a sense of trust and continuity, the current ecological and social crises have increased the sense of contingency, exacerbating the inbuilt anxiety about the unknown future.

The human relationship with the natural world is partly mediated through dwelling. While mobile dwelling of the nomads may have provided a temporary existence, their territorial roots provided continuity and permanence. The modern city reinvents this temporary existence, but seems to deny the sense of rootedness and continuity to many of its inhabitants. Moreover, the increased rate of natural and human disasters, such as floods and wars, has displaced large numbers of people, creating enormous movements of people across countries and continents, living in the most ephemeral of all settlements: refugee camps and tent cities. The tent may be the primary symbol of temporary living, as compared to the house that signifies an aspiration for permanence. The history of architecture starts from nomadic tents, which may be the first time humans attempted to build a structure and lie down roots. Architects see the tent as the prototype of the building, as the first attempt by the humans to construct a shelter, rather than using natural shelters such as forests and caves. It was a sign of confidence to be free from the limitations of the place, and be able to move about freely, exploring the world by foraging bands and setting up tents wherever that food was plentiful.

In response to this nomadism, which has been magnified by modern urban conditions, Heidegger looks for a stable and durable relationship with the land, which he finds in dwelling (Figure 5.8). This connection to permanence is also evident in the idea of genius loci, a spirit of the place that dwells in a place,

FIGURE 5.8 *In the change from the tent to the hut, settled populations established a more permanent relationship with the land (Reconstruction of an early hut, Northumberland, UK).*

reflecting its specific features and unchanging characters (Norberg-Schultz, 1980). Heidegger links being to temporality, which removes the possibility of a permanent essence that precedes existence. It also removes a reliable foundation for the human mind, creating a state of continuous flux and change, and consequently an inherent sense of anxiety. In response, and to look for a reliable foundation for managing anxiety, he looks to externalizing this lost essence onto the material world, hence the desire to be rooted in a place. In the absence of a permanent self, however, a permanent place would not be easily found and could not provide the security that is being sought.

In modern urban living, the relationship between the tent and the house has been projected into the relationship between renting and owning a dwelling, at least in some contexts. Renting, which has grown in size and scope, seems to signify the status of unsettled life. Whereas in some countries renting has been the norm for the settled life, and households may live in the same rented homes for their entire life, in countries that are dominated by the desire for homeownership it has been a problem that needs addressing. Now renting versus owning a dwelling has become a line of division between precariousness and stability. In the United Kingdom, the debate about the rising average age of home ownership is inherently about the instability that faces the renters, as distinct from the owners who can be protected, and be benefiting, from the rising house prices. It is anticipated that by 2025, more than half of those under forty years of age would be renting their homes from private-sector landlords, as the continually rising house prices would prevent them from buying their homes. A generational shift is, therefore, identified, from a generation for whom homeownership was a norm to a 'generation rent', who cannot afford to own their homes anymore (Osborne, 2015).

It is an intergenerational inequality that is taken to be a sign of the passing of a more prosperous and secure time and the entry into the more difficult and unstable years that lie ahead. The governments since the 1980s have promoted the right to own a property as a general principle, the basis on which a 'home owning democracy' can be developed (Maclellan and Osborn, 2015). The conditions of the generation rent, however, show the contradictions of this slogan. While it was used to facilitate the privatization of public and social housing, it has not been sufficient to make homes accessible for those who cannot afford them. Under the conditions that owning a home is an investment for the future, as the most important form of saving for the old age and for family support, forced renting becomes a vulnerability and a sign of inequality. Renting, therefore, becomes a new version of nomadism, which may be welcome by some people at some stage of their lives, but not commonly expected to be a permanent feature of living. If renting is not supported to offer long-term security, it only induces instability and insecurity. Renting becomes a key feature of temporary urbanism, in which attachment to homes and neighbourhoods is threatened by short-term living and continuous pressures to move to new places. Precarity in the social and natural environments becomes the primary implication of temporary urbanism.

Conclusion

Accelerated temporality generates a sense of uncertainty and anxiety, caused by a disconnection from certainties which were thought to have been timeless and embodied in the natural world. The place of the natural environment in our sense of time is significant, so the rising extent of fragility in the planet's material structure contributes to generating a heightened perception of transience, and with it a desire for reconnection and security. The historical sense of continuity is no longer certain and radical changes have threatened the legacies of the past with extinction. The analysis of the attitude to the past, which was explored in the previous chapter in the city, can be extended to the natural environment, which shows how what seemed to be permanent now seems fragile and exposed to the possibility of annihilation, and how its survival is based on continual remaking.

Approaching the natural world has often been paradoxical, showing the ambiguous relationship between humanity and the planet. The natural world has been understood as ordered and harmonious, as well as wild and diverse, a range of attitudes that merely reflect our own conditions and states of mind. Nature within human body and mind and in the environment surrounding us has been acknowledged to change, but also providing a stable foundation on which to construct a sense of trust and permanence. However, with the loss of confidence, the interpretation of the nature within has moved from unity to multiplicity, undermining the possibility of stable meaning and continuous identity. The interpretation of the nature without has also changed from a wild beast to be conquered and transformed into a fragile subject of increasing concern. Examples of this fragility are found in natural disasters, such as earthquakes and floods, which can transform or even demolish a city in a very short period of time: interim cities after major disasters, such as refugee camps, or dislocations caused by climate change. This chapter has shown how the concern for the natural environment shares its outlook with the historical romantic attitude, which emerged in response to modernity and looked to the past as the source of value, and which has now been revived in the context of environmental fragility. Both these changes fuel the inherent sense of anxiety about the future, which no longer can be addressed by being rooted in a place. The state of nature tends to turn permanence into contingency and temporariness. Can there be any creative potential in change and contingency? This is the question to which we now turn.

PART THREE

Experimental Temporality

After investigating the instrumental construction of time and its largely negative impacts on the existential dimensions of society and nature, this part looks for the creative potentials of temporary urbanism and their implications for the future of the city.

6

Events and Prospects

So far, we have seen how concepts and institutions have been created to give a logical sense and a degree of predictability to practices and events, and how global modernity tends to unsettle the drive for continuity and stability inherent in these arrangements, by throwing everything into the air, so as to make new arrangements that would make them faster and more profitable. We have also seen the impact of this unsettling, which has caused anxiety about the future, a sense of precarity, and a break with memory, and with the ideas of identity and nature. These chapters have shown a tension between the stability of imagination and experience, the pressure for more fluidity and the existential contingency of material conditions. We have seen how short-lived events can contribute to the acceleration of life imposed by global beats, and be a pragmatic response to structural crises. In this chapter, we look for innovative possibilities of temporary urbanism, beyond consumerism or regressive instrumentalism. In what ways can temporary urbanism contribute to a progressive urban agenda? Can it provide the possibility of innovation that is socially useful rather than merely economically instrumental? Does it have a creative potential, and if so how can it be revealed and mobilized? Are there ways in which the future of cities might benefit from temporary urbanism? This chapter concentrates on experimental temporality as being both diverse and future-oriented, and how temporary interventions may act as catalysts for change.

The chapter will investigate the creative potentials of temporary urbanism in three broad sections: how it questions the status quo through displacement and the break-up of structures, which change perspectives and indicate structural change; how it contributes to the creation of times and spaces of possibility, in particular the opportune times and the public space; and how it can be significant in the processes of making space, in particular through the involvement of civil society forces in alternative practices. In Chapter 3, we have seen what innovation in technical and economic terms might mean and how it would contribute to temporal acceleration. In this chapter, my aim is to identify the innovative and creative potentials of temporary urbanism in areas beyond economic considerations, without losing sight of its possible shortcomings.

Questioning: Displacement and structural transformation

A creative potential of temporary urbanism may lie in its capacity to raise questions: its drive for displacement, which changes perspectives, and the resistance against the structures and hierarchies of power, which transforms practices.

Short-lived events may be considered an ingredient of the evolution and transformation of structures or an *alternative* to permanent structures. In the former case, they may be seen as intervals in structural transformation, as the signs of the structural breakdown and the formation of new structures. As general patterns collapse, through decay or explosion, a series of particular events with no clear overall pattern may emerge, indicating a number of possible futures. Those events that lead to preferred futures would then be considered to be innovative. In the latter case, in contrast, events may be seen as the primary form of temporality, taken to be the principal feature of temporal ontology. General patterns and structures are either questioned or completely ignored, instead emphasizing the multiplicity of temporal fragments as the essence of reality. In this sense, every event is an innovation, as no event is ever repeated and no two events may be the same. Depending on each perspective, innovation may find a completely different set of meanings.

Ultimately, innovation is a value judgement about an event, which would be based on our ontology, epistemology and methodology. This judgement would depend on what we think the world is made of: element or structures, or a combination of them, in which the general and the particular are mixed in a variety of ways. Innovation may be a change in the rules or general patterns, or variation in particular events. How we get to know the world could range from immediate experience to intuition and intellectual processes. Here innovation would reside in a change of perspective, which could transform the way we feel or think about something. How we engage with the phenomena would also vary from going with the flow or trying to shape the future. Innovation here would range from being immersed in a new flow of events, or being able to transform the course of events.

Displacement and change of perspective

Many works of contemporary art are examples of the practices of displacement. By their critical attitude, they challenge the existing beliefs and practices through acts of displacement. By creating unusual shapes and objects, or by locating them in unfamiliar contexts, these works are engaged in an act of critical inquiry, challenging the status quo, showing what might happen if things were not done in the usual manner. The place that is allocated to people and objects is the result, and a constituting element, of the social processes that make up the status quo. A place, therefore, is a framing expression of power over individuals, groups and the material world that mediates between them. By questioning this place through displacement, these social processes and conventions are opened up for fresh inquiry. Displacement becomes an act of critique, a negation of the status quo that could change settled perspectives and trigger the imagination to search for alternative arrangements. In this sense, displacement is not necessarily offering solutions but questioning the conventional ways of seeing, as famously put by John Berger (1977). The creative potential of temporary events does not necessarily lie in their ability or claim of offering long-term and new answers but only to question the previously failed ones.

The urge for change, and the push for revolt against the settled habits and arrangements, is an inherent feature of modernity. While a conservative attitude accepts and even celebrates these settled habits and arrangements, hoping to reproduce them in whole or in part, the modern attitude is critical, demanding a continuous or even a total rethinking of these arrangements, always searching for new ways. These new ways are justified on the basis of their functionality and rationality, or their desirability and sensual appeal. They may also be justified on the basis of improving the conditions of individuals, groups or societies. Whatever the basis of justification, the existing conditions are always questioned through a critical attitude. The critical attitude and the urge for change are the two sides of the same coin, one justifying and supporting the other.

Displacement of an object, moving it away from its usual context and placing it in an unfamiliar one, generates a state of instability, which questions the status quo, and contributes to the fluidity of ideas and practices (Figure 6.1). At once, it challenges the structures and contributes to the development of temporary urbanism. If the works of art were once created to survive for centuries and celebrate continuity and permanence of political and cultural institutions of church and state, now art installations are dismantled after the exhibition and what remains is only a representation, a trace, a memory of the artwork. The ephemerality of the artwork becomes a critique of rigid institutions as well as a reflection and a celebration of the ephemerality of contemporary life. The creative potential of displacement is at once an invitation to questioning the status quo and exploring alternative perspectives (Figure 6.2).

FIGURE 6.1 *Street art is a prime example of the potential for critical displacement (Vienna, Austria).*

FIGURE 6.2 *Visitors to an exhibition are invited to participate by choosing a ladder of their choice, indicating that their preference for the size and material of the ladder would determine their entrance to the future (Beijing, China).*

Structural transformation

In addition to displacement that could change perspectives and show new pathways, temporary events may also indicate structural change, as both reflecting and initiating an alternative to the established temporal structures, with their associated material and institutional arrangements. Short-lived events, in other words, could anticipate and initiate a major process of restructuring. They may be the signs of large structures collapsing, broken into many pieces and therefore opening the way for new formations to emerge. They may not have the force of restructuring, but only be the symbols of structural transformation. Alternatively, the accumulation of temporary events may gather a force that would transform established structures.

A moment of structural break-up tends to generate a degree of anxiety as well as hope about the future. It may be thought to be a moment of liberation from obsolete or unjust constraints. The moment of the break-up could be the place of promise for new beginnings; a point from which a number of possible futures may be pursued. It provides the conditions of possibility for radical change, which can take any number of directions. The break-up offers the idea and the possibility of emancipation from the limitations of the present, from the undesirable and potentially unfair conditions of a particular circumstance. This is why the nineteenth century witnessed an overlap of romantic and revolutionary movements, combining hope and anger to construct utopian dreams. Hope dominates and anxiety is pushed to the background, as the future is being recast in the elemental dust caused by the break-up of the existing structures.

The causes of structural break-ups may be theorized in different ways. In Hegel's thought, it is a clash of opposites that causes the emergence of a new synthesis, all moving in the direction of progress and sophistication. In Marx's account, which follows Hegel's, this progressive movement is caused by the internal contradictions of the system, which pulls it apart by the necessity of the scientific laws of history. In Lenin's account, such transformation is also accelerated by the avant-garde, which ensures that the leadership for structural break-up is ready at hand. In biological accounts of structural change, which prefer evolution to revolution, as exemplified by the systems theory and the Chicago School of Sociology, it is caused by gradual changes and adjustments, which at some point translate to a sudden structural transformation, or by outside shocks to a system that transmute it. In evolutionary economics of Schumpeter, it is caused by the internal dynamics of the system that periodically renews itself. The break-up of a structure, therefore, is thought to be caused by its internal dynamics which entailed its change, or by external pressures that break it apart.

Meanwhile, critics such as poststructuralists and empiricists may doubt even the existence of such structures, therefore aiming at re-imagining the ontology of the world as pure multiplicity. The problem becomes accounting for change if such structures did not exist. Foucault (2008:3), for example, starts from 'the decision that universals do not exist', which leads him to 'asking what kind of history we can do'. His question becomes, 'How can you write history if you do not accept a priori the existence of things like the state, society, the sovereign, and subjects?'

The possible pathways that open up after a major change, whether or not through the destruction of a structure, however, are not entirely unprecedented or decontextualized. The possible pathways do not appear out of nowhere, and moving into any of those paths may be by choice, but also by necessity. When choices are made, they may not be a free movement in a chosen direction, as they would ultimately be limited by the context and conditions. In the open field, however, the landscape of power is not a level-playing field. Its routes are already mapped by history, geography and social institutions; its character is already shaped by the previous activities and memories of the place. Its current operations are dominated by stronger players: economically by the large corporations that can operate in multiple locations around the world; politically by the state institutions and organized interests; and culturally by deeply rooted institutions and those who have privileged access to the infrastructure of communication and can articulate their demands in the name of rationality and public interest. There are, therefore, underlying traces and forces at work, which can influence and shape the conditions of possibility of change.

The future, however, is not pre-determined by these maps and traces. Whether through the break-up of structures or through gradual change, unforeseen events and new directions are always possible. In other words, an event cannot be reduced to the conditions of its possibility; and so determinism should be avoided in analysing temporary events. The interaction between the deep frameworks, remnants of the dismantled structures and everyday events becomes the driving force of change. The outcome would be influenced by many different forces, which makes predicting the future an almost impossible task, always limited to extrapolating the current trends. As sceptics such as David Hume had argued, however, there is no guarantee that what has happened so far would continue in the future. In logical terms, it is no more than a highly contingent, inductive generalization.

What are the impacts of shattering structures on temporality? Structures of power and habit create particular patterns of temporality, as institutionalized in quantitative time. Routines of work, travel and rest in and between locations that are specified with particular functions generate the fixed spatial-temporal structure of the city. When these structures are crushed, they are replaced by a move towards a multiplicity of temporalities and life trajectories. The routines of the new city are far more individualized than before, generating the conditions of temporal multiplicity. As the higher frequency of temporary events signal structural change, they also indicate the possibility of innovation through the creation of new formations, new perspectives, and new courses of action.

In the break-up of any existing structures, new paths may be opened into a number of different directions. The existing frameworks are shattered and out of their ruins the construction of a new landscape becomes possible. The new landscape may offer opportunities for change that would improve the lives of many people. This break-up may alternatively lead to a completely unexpected, and potentially negative, result, dismantling the hard-earned achievements of a group or society. In a non-linear history, such a break-up is no longer a guarantee for progress, as it was thought to be in the linear accounts of historical change, where the future was always more advanced than the past and history marched forwards. In contrast, a major structural change could be a step backwards into ignorance and poverty, beyond the control of those who are affected by it. The critical attitude that would merely dismantle an arrangement without providing a viable alternative could simply open the way for the powerful players and the forces of creative destruction. In other words, the question is: in a playing field dominated by strong players, who is likely to benefit from the fluidity of the circumstances? Does it exacerbate the conditions of precarity for the vulnerable of the conditions of innovation for the strong? Displacement and structural break-up may therefore change established perspectives and introduce alternative practices. Their creative potential lies in questioning the existing ways of seeing and doing, opening up new possibilities and directions, which may move in any number of directions.

Experimenting: Times and spaces of possibility

The second area in which the creative potential of temporary urbanism may be explored is in its capacity for experimenting with ideas and practices, and the way the concepts of time and innovation may change themselves. In this case, the times and spaces of possibility become significant: moments and locations in which events can be pursued on an experimental basis.

Events and moments: From Chronos to Kairos

Temporary urbanism is the range of short-term actions and events which take place *in time*, but their *timing* may not be in line with the predictable patterns of quantitative time. They may appear to run counter to the highly regulated structures of time and the expectable temporal patterns and routines of the city. In this respect, they may be considered as the examples of Kairos, the occasional and qualitative time.

The two concepts of Chronos and Kairos represented two ways of thinking about time in ancient Greece. Some have referred to Kairos as unregulated time, as 'occasion', in contrast to the regulated idea of time that is expressed through Chronos. But Kairos is itself an interpretation of a set of circumstances, which is considered to be opportune; if it is taken to mean the 'right time', it adds a layer of significance: it is not any occasion but one in which particular things may happen. It is not a mere accident that shows the randomness of the world but a moment which offers new possibilities that may be used instrumentally. This is why it has also been translated as opportunity. In other words, among the many moments that make up our lives, some are special moments, when events can take new directions and new outcomes may emerge. Moments may be ordinary, but only some stand out as the times of possibility. It seems to be these moments that are called Kairos. In a sense, the creative potential of temporary urbanism may lie in a search for these moments, in which new directions and opportunities may occur.

The distinction between Chronos and Kairos is between quantitative and qualitative time. The notion of moment, as the point that separates a before from an after, has been used as an alternative to the historiography that is based on permanent and long, slow processes of historical change. While Chronos is slow and long-term temporality, Kairos is 'the opening of a discontinuity in a continuum' (quoted in Jordheim, 2007:127). It is 'a particular and exceptional moment, a rupture or a turning point, either in the sense of the right or the favourable moment, to speak or to act, or with reference to a particularly decisive, fateful or dangerous situation' (Jordheim, 2007:127). History is then interpreted as a series of ruptures and decisive moments, rather than a continuous process of change. This is evident in the theory of paradigm shifts (Kuhn, 1970) or epistemic ruptures (Foucault, 1989; 2002; Madanipour, 2011). Kairos is characterized by change, conflict, fate and individuality, and as such is in contrast to logos, the dominant pattern of thought in the West, which emphasizes timelessness, form, law, stasis and method (Tillich, quoted in Jordheim, 2007:130). As Walter Benjamin wrote, 'History is the subject of a structure whose site is not homogeneous, empty time, but time filled by the presence of the now [*Jetztzeit*]' (Benjamin, 1999:252–3). The 'now-time' or *Jetztzeit* would therefore point to the potential for change that is inherent in the historical situation, and to the image of the present projected onto the past. The relationship between Chronos and Kairos, between time and chance, is depicted in different ways by the artists. While Rubens depicts them to be friends, others tend to show them at the opposite ends of a struggle: the rapid movement of time prevents people from grasping their chance (Wittkower, 1938).

Temporary urbanism may be interpreted as emphasizing Kairos rather than Chronos, formed of moments and ruptures, rather than continuities and certainties. The question is whether it amounts to a single moment of decisive action, or it is more likely to be made of many moments, with varying degrees of significance. Rather than fateful moments, it may be a collection of everyday ruptures. Can the totality of these ruptures be a contributor to, and a symptom of, a larger structural rupture? If so, what are its implications?

Movement and change could be a threat as well as an opportunity. In response to the flows of time which may transform things without paying any attention to the context, spatiality seems to offer a sense of embeddedness and contextuality. Foucault (1993) criticized the prevalence of time and process, seeing it as the rule of causality and hierarchy; instead, he advocated space and its simultaneity as a form of freedom, whereby things do not follow from one another in any particular order but coexist and may or may not correlate. Similarly, Deleuze advocated a nomadic mode of thought, which was not bound by norms and conventions, but was free to move in many different directions (Deleuze and Guattari, 1994; Patton, 2010). However, undermining time and process, and ignoring the context-dependent nature of thought and action, may also mean undermining the possibility of movement and change, and praising space on its own may mean praising fixity and rigidity. Due weight is, therefore, needed to be given to both time and space, as the two parameters of our experience, as the possibility of both simultaneity and change.

Disruption and transformation

Badiou (2005; 2009) articulates a notion of event as an unusual rupture that has major consequences. As Žižek (2014:179) writes, 'In capitalism, where things have to change to remain the same, the true Event would have been to transform the very principle of change.' For Badiou, events are the major turning points, after which things are not the same as before; events such as falling in love, a new movement in the arts, a new scientific discovery, or a major political revolution. They are novel occurrences that have no previous designation. He calls the consequences of these events, and the transmission of their meaning, as truth; the way they are described and how they have an impact on the following course of life. Following Badiou, Žižek develops this line of thought on events. As he describes an event 'at its purest and most minimal: something shocking, out of joint, that appears to happen all of a sudden and interrupts the usual flow of things; something that emerges seemingly out of nowhere, without discernible causes, an appearance without solid being as its foundation' (Žižek, 2014:2). This change can be in the way we perceive things, or a change in things themselves: a change of perspectives or a change of material reality.

This analysis limits what can be considered as an event to major occurrences that introduce a turning point in the normal course of life. In our analysis, however, the subject matters are not the single events of considerable significance, but a series of smaller events, which are recognizable by their higher frequency and shorter length. The subject of analysis includes but is not limited to the event, but also encompasses ordinary events. Badiou and Žižek articulate a notion of event as an unusual rupture that has major consequences. They limit what can be considered as an event to occurrences that introduce a turning point in the normal course of life. In concentrating on life-changing events, they tend to ignore the everyday events that may cause small changes that may not even be initially detectable. These events are the building blocks of reality, but if they are excluded from investigation as banal or unimportant, something significant may be missed. Events, large or small, significant or inconsequential, are the basis of ontology, and if we exclude the majority of these events, how can we say that we are analysing life? If we want to pay attention to them, how do we analyse these events?

A key feature of capitalism is the urge for continuous change so as to remain competitive. The dilemma for the analysis of temporary urbanism, which seems to be about the acceleration of the pace of change, is therefore to see whether it is merely an intensification of the workings of capitalism, or it has also a creative potential beyond such considerations. Capitalism is eager on disruptive events only if they lead to higher economic productivity and bigger returns on investment, if they transform and remove the obstacles that are in the way of such accumulation. However, its flexibility is exercised within a clearly defined system of rules and regulations, protecting particular forms of controlling property and performing behaviour. As a result, it strongly defies the disruptive interventions that would go against this system and its economic logic. For example, the demands for environmental protection and care may be seen as a negative disruption in a system that is fully flexible towards disruptions that are aligned with profit maximization. Therefore, not all disruptive interventions may have the same meaning and implications; it would all depend on their context, orientation and possible outcome.

Events can be about a change in reality, or a change in the perspectives with which we understand and explain reality. If there is a sudden change in the way we perceive the world, so that we can see the world with new eyes, we may call it an event. The examples of this can be found in people who solve a problem by looking at it from a different angle, or those who embrace a new belief, whereby the same reality is understood in a different way. Such radical changes of perspective open a new horizon before our eyes, portraying a completely different picture of the same scene. This may bring about major innovations in an individual or a society's life, whereby tomorrow will be very different from yesterday. The radical change of perspective is one of the main forms of innovation, which is facilitated through the meeting of minds, through interaction between different perspectives that are open to change.

But this notion of event sees it as a life-changing occurrence. If events become the common currency of social life, as in a trend such as temporary urbanism, how can they be interpreted? Life-changing events may still signal the turning points in our life, but what if we have many small turning points in a condition in which change is the primary form of experience? Are we engaged in frequent changes of perspective? If we do, what is the impact of such frequency on our sense of ourselves and others? Can we keep a perspective, a belief, for a while, or do we live in a situation of flux? What would innovation mean under such conditions of the rapid changes of perspective, where fluidity rather than fixity is the norm, and where novelty may wear off as soon as it has arrived? Under such conditions, nothing can stand still, and the creative potential of a change in perspective may be overwhelmed by the rapidity and scale of change. This is particularly evident in the speed of technological change, whereby the attitude towards reality changes with every new technological innovation. Under such conditions, perspectives and attitudes are continually changing, and the creative potential of temporariness lies in itself, that is, it is temporariness as such that counts as innovative, rather than the innovations that keep coming to the stage.

Small events and systemic change

The interface between events and laws, and the impact of small events on major systemic change has been analysed as changes within a system or in interaction with the surrounding environment. Darwin's theory of evolution focuses on change through interaction with the environment, drawing on a combination of variation and adjustment. There is a wide range of variations among the members of any species; those features that are better adaptable to the environment will be passed on to the next generation; as a result, the species will evolve to have a better chance of survival. In any life form, there is a large range of variation, where new genetic mutations may be caused by random mistakes, creating new varieties that may be better or worse in adapting to the environment. In this way, change occurs in nature not as a result of repetition of the same, but of the occurrence of the slightly different. In natural evolution, deviation from routine may therefore be an absolutely necessary ingredient in the survival of species, in which mistakes and accidents that occur in the process of reproduction strengthen the likelihood of survival by broadening the field of possibilities. The lack of adjustment to the environment and the absence of diversity would lead to the demise of a species, whereas flexibility and random variation would increase its chances of survival. There are interesting parallels between the processes of change in the natural and the social worlds in terms of flexibility and diversity. Can the same logic be extended to the social life? Can temporary events be considered as experiments in social evolution?

In social life, according to this interpretation, mistakes and unforeseen events would be an integral part of innovation and social change. If societies remained completely static by always repeating the same routines, their ability to adapt to the changing circumstances would suffer and it may even lead to their demise. Yet the society and its environment are both continually changing. Variation and adjustment may therefore be as important in the social as well as the biological survival. While rigid routines may freeze a society in a particular timeframe, its own dynamics and the environment in which it lives will have moved on. For the group or the society to survive, it needs to fill the gap that has been created through the mismatch between a rigid constitution and a changing context. The disruption caused by non-routinized events may be interpreted as an essential ingredient in the process of adjustment to the environment. The accidents, disasters and mistakes; the increased variation in the features of society by the transfer of new ideas, practices and people, will all have a role to play in this constructive disruption.

There are, however, at least two problems in such a comparison: time and agency. The problem of time refers to the different timespans in which the biological and social changes take place. It makes it very dangerous to extend the biological theories, with their very long processes of transformation, to social life with its much limited timespan, which in comparison may only appear as just a fleeting moment. If random events in social life are accidental or by mistake, they may open up new spaces for experimentation and adjustment, repetition and difference, which may have previously been non-existent or ignored. But the opportunities for adjustment to the environment, which may take place generations, centuries and millennia in biological processes, are not afforded to social change. The second problem is that of agency. The difference between the natural and social processes may be that one is based on multiplication and adjustment, whereas the other would also include protest, planning and appraisal. In society, protest or planned action may lead to events that are not a mistake or an accident, but a purposeful endeavour to institute change. Rather than repeating the past, these innovations are driven by a desire for change, rather than by random genetic mutation. Whereas change in biological evolution is driven by the multiplication of new varieties and the demise of ill-adjusted variations, in social life there is also a conscious desire for change. The reproduction of a society may take place through innovation and adjustment, but if it is fundamentally an unjust society it will be subject to challenge by its members for radical rather than adaptive change.

Human agency and limited temporality, therefore, would make the comparison untenable. And yet, there are always lessons for human societies by observing the natural life processes. In the context of our investigation, it offers the observation that vitality lies not only in protective measures but also in disruptive ones; not only in routines and repetitions, but also in events and accidents; not only in permanent arrangements that guarantee stability and endurance, but also in temporary interventions that introduce variation and flexibility.

Temporary events may also be analysed according to the systems theory and chaos theory. In these theories, an event is an integral part of a system, and even if it appears to be random, it may have structural effects. As discussed earlier in this chapter, events may be signs of structures crumbling or new ones emerging; here we see how events may start a process of structural change. Temporary events may be considered as experiments or accidents that could lead to structural change. As the famous example of the butterfly effect in chaos theory suggests, an event may not have an apparent consequence, but it can trigger a chain of events that could lead to significant changes. Even though these theories of evolution and chaos open up some space for random events, they both try to bring them under a certain level of regularity. The system prevails over the individual acts, and the possibility of creativity is a mere illusion in a highly ordered system, even if the system is far more flexible than it had been imagined before.

Spaces of contingency and recognition

One of the ways of overcoming the paralysis of multiplicity and the demise of structure is to develop the spaces of possibility, in which the different temporal fluxes can coincide and interact. If self is a void in which different forces interact, public space is the external equivalent of this void for the city, where its identity is shaped through the interaction of different forces in the public domain. It is a place which facilitates the possibility of different events, through which the city's character and identity, and the shape of its future, are made. Public spaces are crossroads, as Alberti (1988) noted; as such they are the spaces of contingency, expression and recognition. While events and experiments can take place in almost any place, it is in public spaces that they become noticed and shared, if they are ever to acquire social significance.

Public space by definition is a place of temporary activities (Figure 6.3). It is a place of events, which are almost always short-lived. Events follow each other and people come and go, as no one is expected or allowed to stay in the public environment for long. Even those who remain in the public space for long hours, such as street traders, and the homeless who have no choice but to live on the street, do not stay on the same spot for long. The public space, therefore, may not be flexible in form and its spatial arrangement, but it is often flexible in its content, allowing different people to be present and different activities to take place for a short period of time. As a place of movement and repose, it houses people who pass through and those who

FIGURE 6.3 *Public space is by definition the place of temporary events (York, UK).*

stay for a while. It is a place of social meetings, competition and conflict, and performance and communication. But those who are involved eventually move on to other places and activities, in turn replaced by others, who may have equal claim to presence in the public environment. In this sense, public space is the space of social life, which is multifarious and constantly changing and evolving (Madanipour, 2003; 2010).

Public space, in all its different forms and shades of publicness, therefore, is the space of possibility and consequence, in which many different forms of short-term events may find expression and may lead to other events. Public space is the constructor and container of events, their space and condition of possibility, and at the same time it is constructed by events, both predictable and unpredictable. It is the place in which events are disclosed and become public, or at least publicly visible, and thereby starting a possible chain of actions and reactions that may not be completely predictable or controllable. As a place of experimentation, it is often the place of small and everyday events and processes, but it is occasionally the place of major events that may change the course of social life in a city. As a crossroad and an open field, it is the stage on which public life unfolds, with all its diverse phenomena and their multiple meanings; the field of social encounter, political contest, cultural communication and economic exchange (Figure 6.4). All these

FIGURE 6.4 *For a few days over the summer, the travelling fair creates a temporary space for social encounters at the heart of the city (Newcastle, UK).*

activities and experimentations can take place in many specialized places in the urban environment, but it is in the public space that the possibilities for unpredictable, intersubjective events are highest.

The public space, however, may not be an entirely open field, as it includes elements of physical and institutional fixity. In cities, public spaces are defined by fences, buildings and other ways of enclosing a place and separating it from other places. In older parts of cities, it is often the buildings that surround the crossroad that define this public space (Alberti, 1988). As a meeting place, its existence is largely recognized by the boundaries that define it. Many images of the most famous public spaces of the world will inevitably include some of the buildings that surround them. These buildings frame the public space, carving it out of the larger urban fabric. The fixity of the surrounding boundaries, therefore, is an integral part of the ephemeral sense of openness that public spaces offer. The two senses of fixity and flexibility go hand in hand. It is not possible to separate the fixed from the flexible, the permanent from the ephemeral. The façade of the buildings, the opening of streets, doorways and passages into the public space are all parts of the flow of life into and out of it, as well as the spaces and activities that frame this space of possibility. The frame shapes the conditions that create a space of possibility and multiplicity.

Public spaces take many forms and there are public spaces that are less clearly delimited by their surroundings. Beyond those urban spaces that are architecturally well-articulated, public spaces of open fields and parks may have a more fluid and ambiguous relationship with what surrounds them. But even these places are not floating and free from restriction. They are defined by their location, conditioned by their relationship with the territory on which they are located. Fixity may not be based on the walls and building facades that frame a space, but on the shape and conditions of land on which the space is developed and experienced. This may be a more primordial form of relationship between a fixed framework and a flexible content. Here too, framework and content are intertwined, not easily separable. The relationship to the land is equally applicable to the urban public spaces, making them doubly framed within two forms of fixity: that which surrounds them and that which lies underneath them. It is in this relation to land that a sort of permanence is sought, looking for the spirit of the place or the historical roots of identity. Land, rather than buildings, offers a far deeper sense of fixity.

Any fixities, from the buildings that surround it to the objects that may be found in it, from the facades of the buildings to the statues of rulers and heroes, and to trees and fountains, are often few in number. Their presence reflects the purposeful decisions as well as accidents; the power of higher authorities, the individual encroachments, the unintended traces of urban development and the remains of the past. Beyond these fixities, however, the public space, in its different forms and sizes, is the place of short-lived events, where routines are played out and casual happenings take place. Fixities within it would mean staking a claim to the space, and as the space is theoretically belonging to everyone, it is a place that is characterized by the relative absence of fixities, even if unfolding within strict routines, traditions and laws.

Fixities, however, are not limited to being spatial and corporeal, but they are also institutional and technological, which frame the public space and limit its possibility of experimentation, without being visible. Social norms, rigid rules of conduct and the pressure for surveillance may not populate the public space with fixed objects, and therefore allow the space to be felt as a place of temporary and experimental activities. But it is highly regulated, and its neatness and emptiness may be a witness to this regulation. Without it, public space may indeed become a place of permanence for those forces that can claim it for their purposes. The reason for the gradual shrinkage of medieval public spaces was this encroachment by private interests, leaving the public space to the absolute minimum that was possible within the city walls (Saalman, 1968). However, while these pressures are always present, other pressures remain to keep the space open for temporary activities, as it is in these activities that social life becomes possible. When fixities become material and take external shape, it is when the pressure has been sufficiently strong to stake its claim permanently, hence the appearance of the statues and monuments, which are claims for power, order and control of contingency.

While public space may offer the possibility of temporary activities, based on experimentation and the freedom from fixed functions, it is not a space of complete freedom. It is a conditioned space, in which some experiments will be tolerated while others frowned upon, prohibited or even punished. Public space, therefore, offers a limited possibility of freedom, so it does not deliver an extended promise of emancipation. Some activists, such as the Situationists, thought of temporary actions in public space as a sign of freedom (Debord, 1994). For them, politics and aesthetic come together in the moment of protest in public space. But even they abandoned this illusion, as it was clear that society was organized on an institutional basis that could not be transformed by spontaneous gestures in public spaces (McDonough, 2002). These gestures could challenge certain beliefs and rules but could not change the fundamental rules that reproduce society. The likes of flaneurs, drifters and others could question the ordered spaces but could not change them substantially. The roots of capitalism or the political institutions of power, for example, are so well established that they could not be reached by temporary gestures and spontaneous displays of difference. If the system was well ingrained, challenging it needed much stronger tools than small movements.

Nevertheless, it is in the public space that power is displayed and challenged. Public space is a substantive challenge to the procedural and discursive ideas of urbanism. It produces the material conditions in which the citizens can improve their lives. Also, it is a political challenge to authoritarian arrangements; it provides the possibility of unplanned events, albeit within a social framework. This is why the temporary events could offer a limited possibility of emancipation, as it is not tightly fitted within the prearranged rules, but it is potentially an expression of freedom.

The primary political meaning of space is power. Whoever is in charge of the urban space is in charge of the society. This is why in coup d'états and revolutions, the urban space and the key public institutions are the target of control, and why these spaces have been the spaces of presentation by statues of leaders, military parades and religious rituals. A protest is a challenge to this status of power. Democratic politics frames and institutionalizes conflict, taming the protest so as to make it an ordinary event. But in undemocratic and inflexible situations, protest stands outside the system and threatens it. The use of urban space for protest, therefore, is an indication of the failure of the political institutions to offer democratic openings to dissenting voices. The political protest in public space can also affect the relations between social groups by demanding recognition through making the invisible visible.

Recognition, as many thinkers since Hegel have argued (Habermas, 1989; 1984; Taylor, 1994; Honneth, 1995; Ricoeur, 1995; 2007;), is a powerful social force. It is a part of a struggle for status that is an engine of social processes (Weber, 1978; Bourdieu, 2000). Temporary events as public gestures for asserting status and demanding recognition, therefore, would lie at the heart of the way society works. As diversity has intensified and social institutions have become more flexible and fluid, the urge for recognition has become more urgent than ever before for many social groups. Recognition becomes an integral part of an emancipatory process, in which marginalized social groups can claim a stake and change the perspectives of the others towards themselves (Figure 6.5).

Large protests in urban spaces are a combination of places and events. Places and events are neither singular nor occurring in a void. Both are rooted in particular contexts, physically and socially. The protest is not a single event, but many events over a period of time, a culmination of many processes, and it may continue in different forms, and in the context of national and international politics. The place is also not singular or accidental. It is part of a network of urban spaces. It tends to be selected for an already existing symbolic meaning, where a demonstration can be most visible and effective.

FIGURE 6.5 *Protests, festivals and other gatherings in public spaces contribute to the construction of shared meaning and a sense of solidarity (Durham, UK).*

It has a history, and people have a memory of that place. But a political protest may behave like a flood, forcing its way into any significant opening or even destroying some places to flow. When the place and the event are joined, space can become an integral part of the action as its originator, facilitator (space, media, internet), stage (space) and even target (demand for freedom, for institutional and physical public space).

The public spaces that have become famous for protest movements stand as an icon for these movements. Places such as Taksim in Istanbul and Tahrir in Cairo work as monuments to a cause (Figure 6.6). To become a monument, they are subject to a process of representation and reception. Those who are involved use the space as the symbol of their gathering, even if it may have happened in a number of different places. It is like any process of icon-making, the production of monumentality with all its positive and negative implications. On the one hand, those involved generate a story around an experience, an image, a place, by living it, telling it and showing it. On the other hand, others subscribe to this story, accepting it as part of their memory. It is an exchange in the economy of attention mediated by the social media and the news media. The difference between a social image and a commercial one is that one is based on experience and suffering, the other based on commodities

FIGURE 6.6 *Some places, such as Taksim Square, find a monumental significance in the urban consciousness, even after temporary events (Istanbul, Turkey).*

and manufactured images. Together they create a representation that could stay in the collective memory for long.

Public space is the space of temporary events, which has been outside the fixed private territories, even if parts of public space have been used for fixed objects. The fourth plinth in London's Trafalgar Square is continually the place of a new performance, exemplifying how the idea of fixed monumental objects has also been replaced by transience (Figure 6.7). Urban space reflects an accelerated palimpsest, an intensified creative destruction, in which new activities replace others at high rates, cleaning the slate at unprecedented rates, fitting in with the age of speed and the conditions of disposability. But the slate is not clean; it always has particular characteristics, which shape and condition the possibilities it affords. Affordance of a space depends on its context: where it is located in the city, what legal and institutional constraints it is under, what range of agencies and institutions are involved in its management and maintenance, what historical memories it has in the popular imagination, and so on.

Public space can be the space of possibility that would allow society to be expressed in alternative ways. The routines and settled structures of society

FIGURE 6.7 *Rather than becoming the base for another fixed object, the fourth plinth of Trafalgar Square has been used for a sequence of temporary displays (London, UK).*

are reflected in its social and spatial arrangements, taming and limiting the unpredictable and contingent elements. Its creative potential lies in the sphere of contingency, where the unplanned and unexpected can take place, where the social fragments meet and where some of the hidden or suppressed layers of society can be expressed. These can occur anywhere, but their social manifestations can find the space of development and expression in the public space. Public space becomes the space of consciousness for the urban society, where its suppressed elements and its unconscious can come to light. It can trigger social innovation by becoming the space for alternative existence and alternative expressions.

Construction of meaning

The increasing number of festivals, parades, street performances and various other short-term events may be interpreted as a drive for the commercialization of urban life, as many of these events are associated with some commercial activity. Some events, such as the running competitions through the streets of cities, like the marathons in London, New York and Paris, may be interpreted as elements of city marketing and competition, as cities try to keep up with their competitors and to attract attention. Events that might have had a stronger religious or cultural meaning in the past, such as the preparations for the arrival of Christmas, may now be seen to be primarily geared towards encouraging people to buy more and spend more, changing the meaning of the event from a cultural to a commercial one.

Street lights and decorations in various venues are used as opportunities for the encouragement of consumption. Festival shopping that emerged as a drive for the regeneration of rundown areas, and the construction of atriums and malls that could reproduce a sanitized version of street life, were all signs of an economy driven by retail and entertainment. The tendency to use the public environment for short-term leisure activities, such as the street cafés, were frowned upon until a generation ago in many industrial countries, as signs of laziness and, in any case, unrealistic in cold northerly climates. The growing number of street cafés and restaurants in these cities may be interpreted as the signs of a changing economy and a more epicurean approach to life. The question, therefore, is whether there is any creative potential in these events which goes beyond a merely economic significance.

These examples show how the ephemerality of these events contribute to, and reflect, the increasingly commercial character of the urban society. At the same time, they should not be all reduced to the structural conditions in which they take place. In other words, there may be a wider range of meanings that can be associated with these events. It would be too reductive to read every new activity in the light of structural economic change and commercialization of social life. While there may not be an easy escape from these structural conditions, it is evident that the society is more complex than is assumed; and the pressures to shape it in a particular direction and to offer a particular interpretation of its activities may only succeed to a limited extent. The meaning of ephemeral and short-term events, therefore, would be multiple and diverse (Figure 6.8). A single narrative cannot be the only way in which this flurry of ephemerality can be analysed and interpreted. If we are looking for the creative potential of ephemeral events, we may need to look for an alternative reading of these events. Such a reading may be developed at the level of aesthetic experiment, individual experience and social significance.

At the level of aesthetic experiment, short-term events could provide the opportunity for the generation of new ideas that can be tested in low-risk events. The relationship between artistic creativity and structural economic conditions is by no means causal and direct. Many artistic masterpieces of the past were generated under oppressive conditions, but their meanings were not confined to regressive interpretations, and many were reinterpreted in the subsequent periods in progressive ways. The association of ephemerality

FIGURE 6.8 *Temporary arrangements, such as street decorations, even if driven by consumerism, cannot be reduced to commercial considerations, with some capacity to contribute to the construction of shared meaning (Stockholm, Sweden).*

with accelerated globalization and commercialization of cultural life would not necessarily mean that any artistic work should be interpreted as a representative of these structural conditions. Many aesthetic experiments may be reused in other circumstances towards socially progressive ends and cultural enrichment. Many may also provide a stepping stone for the development of an artistic talent that could be active in other circumstances and towards other ends.

At the level of individual experience, short-term events could contribute to the animation of the urban experience. Lights, decorations and performances could transform a utilitarian and functionalist urban environment into a place of enjoyment. The cultural meaning of such enjoyment may not run deep, but it is a reflection of the fleeting character of the urban cultural meanings, in which the urban experience tends to be a travelling experience. From an urban traveller's perspective, passing through an environment that is enriched through an intensified aesthetic experience may be preferable to one that is austere and functionalist. An experienced urban traveller would not be a passive recipient of the advertising messages and commercial encouragements, but could be a discerning judge in responding to what is on display. Some analysts tend to treat the urban inhabitants as no more than passive and powerless spectators in a commercial urban drama. As skilful adults, however, the spectator is actively engaged with the drama and would have a degree of control on what messages to accept or to ignore. The subliminal effect of the spectacle may transform the cultural habits of the traveller, but the spectacle would have a potentially multi-layered meaning for the spectator.

In terms of social significance, the urban experience would play an important role in the construction of collective meaning in societies in which the older patterns of meaning have declined. The diversity of the population, and the loss of the meaning of older forms of habits and social institutions, would leave an atomized society of individuals with a reduced level of shared meaning. The events in the public domain, whatever their origins, would become vehicles of intersubjective connections and the construction of shared forms of experience and meaning. These shared experiences may be fleeting, and the meaning that is derived from them brief and fragile. When compared to the atomizing forces of functionalist routines, however, any event that goes beyond these routines, no matter how ephemeral, would provide the possibility of constructing a sense of the others. The urban experience, fleeting as it may be, would include others in a collective sense, rather than an introverted travel through the anonymous crowds. When groups of people, large or small, in a major festival or a small street performance, share an experience, they are inherently creating the possibility of the generation of new meaning in social life.

Innovating: Alternative practices

In addition to questioning and experimenting, temporary urbanism may be considered to be a sphere of alternative and innovative practice for the civil society, as distinctive from the forces of the state or market. In other words, it can be the platform for activities that go beyond economic interests and exertion of government control. It is an area in which the space, time and institutions are rethought through alternative practices.

Temporary urbanism may offer the different groups new opportunities for using and creating space in alternative, new ways. This is particularly made possible by the large and small economic crises, which make space available at more affordable prices, but it may also be an indication of a longer term thriftier attitude. The creative potentials of temporary urbanism in socially innovative ways are wide ranging. The artists, civil society groups, charities and community organizations, who had difficulty getting access to space in buoyant property markets, see the oversupply of space as a way of developing community facilities, relations and cultural activities (Figure 6.9). Rather than merely engaging in maximizing returns on investment, individuals and groups, from artists to activists and charities, use space from a different perspective.

FIGURE 6.9 *Empty shops are temporarily used for social purposes (Newcastle, UK).*

They may use empty shops as community hubs, and public spaces for expressing communities' life experiences through the arts, as an alternative to advertising and the display of commercial interests that dominate the public sphere (Figure 6.10).

FIGURE 6.10 *Empty industrial spaces in Via Tortona are converted into temporary exhibition spaces and shops during the annual design week (Milan, Italy).*

The nature of these transformative interventions, however, would depend on the circumstances. Who initiates, what the outcome is, and who benefits are important considerations. While most temporary interventions may be justified with good intentions, the outcome may even be discriminatory, even in the case of civil society actors, who enter a process of bottom-up, innovative and participative actions, reclaiming space for the community. As the subtitle of the American entry for the 2012 Venice Biennale indicated, those who are involved clearly see their work as transforming the urban space in community friendly ways. The key concepts that were expected to pervade the entries for the exhibition were citizenship, protest, equity and participation. But as the organizers also admit, '… *all* of these acts might be gentrification by another name' (Lang Ho, 2013).

Why should these activist spaces trigger gentrification? A primary reason may be the position of the activists and community organizations. Gentrification is the replacement of one socio-economic group with a higher one. It is the result of investment in a place but not in its people, who are then priced out or pushed out. How many of these actions of temporary urbanism are initiated by low-income communities as distinctive from those by middle-class activists? If the middle-income groups occupy the streets of the city to reclaim it from the elite at the top, it does not necessarily mean that they are going to open up the spaces of possibility for the poor. As social inequality has intensified, the ability of the lower income groups to organize themselves and improve their living and working conditions has declined, pushing them further to the margins of society. Environmental improvement actions may respond to the needs of middle-income groups, but not necessarily to those of the marginalized poor, who may lose out in this process (Madanipour et al., 2003; Madanipour, 2010; Madanipour et al., 2014).

The idea of using public spaces for entertainment, which was considered to be an idle pursuit or unfit for cold and rainy northern climates, has now been fully embraced in British cities. It is a testimony to the change in the economic base of the city, and with it the social routines and cultural habits. Design and temporary interventions are used to add colour and life, animating cities as welcoming hosts to the global economy operators, supporting a series of structural changes. Many forms of critique may be interpreted in this light, as an act of Schumpeterian creative destruction, loosening the foundations of a status quo, but feeding its metamorphosis into a new state which may be equally or more exclusive.

Temporary use of space may be seen as a critique of the rigid frameworks of modernist functionalism, with its apparently austere aesthetics and inflexible framework of masterplanning. Masterplanning, however, means different things in different contexts. It is against the old notion of masterplanning that Christopher Alexander (1982) produced his anti-planning vision of incremental growth, which was partly based on the ideas of incremental planning that arose in the United States as a critique of modernist planning (Lindblom, 1959). In the context of discretionary British planning, masterplanning was abandoned decades ago, but it returned as a tool for coordinating the recent construction boom. The Urban Task Force (1999), led by Richard Rogers, argued that masterplanning is the key tool in creating a well-designed, sustainable city. However, during the periods of economic crisis, when the development pressures have disappeared, and the possibility, scale and speed of development are reduced dramatically, a masterplan would become ineffective. In some European contexts, in contrast, masterplanning has never been abandoned and it is a far more fixed arrangement. The notion of temporary urbanism as a critique argues for an experimental form of planning, which loosens this rigidity and opens up a space for experimentation. This critique may also play into the hands of the market, leading to privatization of urban space, creating more freedoms for the private developer. The acts of experimentation through temporary urbanism, however, could also be progressive.

The case of Vorst neighbourhood in Brussels shows the creative potential of temporary urbanism, combining the attempts to change perspective, challenge fixed rules, experimenting with new ideas, and benefiting a low-income community (Figure 6.11). In this case, the local residents were able to use temporary interventions as a catalyst for transformation and demand flexibility from planning restrictions. They were able to overcome the municipal resistance by testing the waters for the successful introduction of a drastic traffic-calming plan that would enable children to walk to school across two pedestrianized squares (Bakker, 2014). The Rotterdam-based firm of designers, Artgineering, worked with the local residents in this lower income neighbourhood, drawing a plan to limit the heavy traffic and street parking that dominated the area. The plan proposed closing off the through traffic and banning street parking, but it was first rejected by the local council, under pressure from a strong car lobby. To change opinion, the local groups involved in the new community centre proposed a temporary intervention, which was carried out by the designers. A group of children, parents, the local women's organization and other supporters occupied the space, cordoning off the square and the crossroads by concrete blocks and large sacks. The sacks were filled on the spot with soil and plants, generating an instant temporary park, which was watered and looked after by the owner of the café at the crossroad. As a result, drivers had to find alternative routes and children were safe to walk to school and play around the new plants. The opponents of the scheme changed their mind and two months later the local council approved the plan. The scheme was selected for the 2014 Dutch Yearbook for landscape architecture and urban design, as the selection committee

FIGURE 6.11 *The creative potential of temporary urbanism is exemplified in the temporary construction of a park, experimenting with ideas and changing perspectives (Brussels, Belgium). Image courtesy of Artgineering, Rotterdam.*

found the design 'attractive and surprisingly inexpensive' and was particularly impressed by the willingness of the designers to show initiative and political engagement (Bakker, 2014:156). The temporary intervention was a catalyst for transformation, facilitating a more permanent arrangement that benefited the local community.

The temporary use of space is a testing of the water for gradual and contingent change, reflecting a pragmatic approach to uncertain circumstances. It becomes a vehicle of innovation for entrepreneurs and start-up businesses. Here again, it is the economics of development that leads the way, which may or may not be sensitive to its social consequences. These attempts for temporary use of space frequently come across resistance by some market operators and public authorities. An empty lot can turn into a useful purpose even if for a few months, but the complaint is that 'Landlords and regulators aren't equipped to handle temporary uses', and that, 'we apply the same licensing burdens, lease agreements, and review processes that are unsuitable for projects that may only last 4 weeks' (Fidler, 2011). Meanwhile, the intended and unintended consequences, and long-term impacts, of temporary interventions remain unclear. The city changes on a case-by-case basis. Each new addition may have its own logic, which may add to the aesthetic richness of the city, but it may also increase other problems as a result of poor coordination. While container architecture may be a fashionable trend and a critique of corporate architecture, it may also reflect lower levels of expectation for the quality of alternative spaces. The results of the 'shoestring buildings and micro-budget parks', as the *Los Angeles Times* architectural critic calls them, may be better than nothing, but their long term impacts on cities are far from clear and agreeable (Hawthorne, 2012).

A temporary state, therefore, may become a stepping stone rather than a stop-gap, going beyond coping with crisis and thinking about what happens next. It offers a sphere of possibility, in which the space offers the widest range of possible new things that can happen, as it has the fewest limits. In a sense, it is like an open field, in which many activities can take place, which makes it ambivalent, as it can be taken into any direction by the interplay of powerful social and economic forces. A temporary activity may act as a transformative medium, helping to create new, or use existing, gaps in an active capacity. It can be used as a catalyst for change, facilitating experimentation, innovation or animation, which can lead to an alternative set of arrangements, which can be socially regressive, such as gentrification, or progressive, such as gaining community advantages.

Conclusion

This chapter has investigated three directions in which the creative potential of temporary urbanism can be explored. A primary capacity of temporary events is raising questions and challenging the status quo, through displacement that could encourage others to see things with different eyes, or by challenging the rigid and oppressive structures, breaking them into smaller temporal and spatial parts. A second area is to develop the spaces and times of possibility for experimentation: moments and events that can turn things round and public spaces that provide the possibility of contingency and unpredictability, triggering the conditions in which experimentation may take place. A third area is the capacity for alternative practices and rethinking institutional arrangements, which enables the civil society and community groups to use and create spaces through alternative processes. In all these three broad areas, we may see how temporary use can play a positive role in the future of cities, helping to transform them in many ways. At each stage, however, I have also tried to show the ambiguity of the process, and the potential for regressive outcomes, such as gentrification or opening up the field to powerful market players. The creative potential of temporary urbanism, therefore, is determined in those cases where social benefits are the outcome of the process, rather than the instrumental acceleration and exploitation of time as a commodity.

7

Cities in Time

This chapter brings together some of the key themes of the book on the implications of ephemerality for the future of cities. It is organized in two sections. The first section addresses the concepts of time and the implications of temporal acceleration and ephemerality for the future of cities. The second section focuses on the categories of temporariness, the creative potential of temporariness for the future of cities and its tensions with the condition of precarity.

Time, acceleration and the city

In our investigation, we have seen how time has been conceptualized in three broad approaches: substantive, relational and intuitive. In each approach, the meaning of time is different, and the impacts of ephemerality and temporal acceleration are differently manifested and evaluated. In many circumstances, however, the three sides of time are all at work to construct the meaning of time, with the tensions and contradictions that may emerge in their interface, and the different visions of the future that may be the outcome.

Substantive time

The first approach is a substantive interpretation of time, which finds expression in the related concepts of essentialist, mechanical and instrumental time. In the essentialist notion, time exists as an independent entity, and events may be interpreted as the instances of this general substance. Many thinkers since Plato have considered time as an independent substance, which may not be seen or touched, but only to be found in the realm of abstract ideas. The basic feature of time is its eternity, and any event or change would be an example, an expression of this eternal, metaphysical substance. Compared to this general, perpetual and abstract framework of time, all events are temporary and particular, mere manifestations of a higher order. The belief in this higher order would make it possible to account for the apparent randomness of the phenomena, as the manifestations of an abstract and permanent substance. Temporariness is a fact of life, from which there is no escape, but which may be overcome through belief in this metaphysical realm of permanence. The perfect form of time is eternity and all events do, or must, point towards this perfection.

In this view, there is a higher realm of Ideas, where there is an abstract idea for each element of the world, which is its perfect form. The proper future path of the city, therefore, would be moving towards this perfect Idea of the city, this utopia. The modern approaches to architecture and planning are often based on a modified version of this substantive view of the world, even if the belief in a realm of pure ideas is not acknowledged. Since the Renaissance, many thinkers have tried to imagine what a perfect city would be like, and designers and planners have tried to move towards this perfect image, to match the reality with the Idea of a good city. Temporariness is inevitable, but it can be a pathway towards this perfect future, or an inconvenient digression that needs to be rectified.

In the mechanical interpretation of this essentialist notion, which was facilitated by the invention of mechanical clocks and was developed into a complete scientific theory by Newton, this abstract time flows at a steady pace and it is an empty container for things and events. For Descartes, who made significant contributions to mathematics, both space and time were substances that could be subdivided and measured. In this essentialist interpretation of time, acceleration or deceleration would not change the core substance of time. Temporal fragments do not have a significance of their own, but are only the surface of a deeper substance that flows at an unchanging pace. In this vision, temporary urbanism would be just another turn of the wheel of time, a mere blip in its speed, an occasional change without any significant substantive effect. It would be measured and charted as a trough on the graph of time, without any impact on the x-y axes that form the framework of measurement. The future of the city is a continuation of its past, showing the movement of a line in the graph, as time flows in a steady pace and in a linear direction of the future.

The essentialist and mechanical notions of time are overlapping with an instrumental concept of time. Time is conceived as a measure of change, quantified and standardized to form a temporal grid superimposed onto the fragments and streams of social life. Essentialized and routinized in a public infrastructure of time made of a series of social institutions and public objects, time is used to tame change and manage society. Reified, regulated and quantified time is locked into spatial arrangements, while abstract, fixed and controlled space is intimately linked with the abstract and quantified time. With the emergence of an economic frame of mind in the modern period, reified time is turned into an asset, with a monetary value, expected to be maximized through speed and multiplication. Time becomes a machine striven to work ever faster and with more precision, pulling into its grip larger numbers of people from around the world, to become cogs in this expanding grid and to keep up with, and help speeding up, its accelerating beats.

In this context, temporary events reveal the tensions and ambiguities in the relationship between the grip of this temporal infrastructure and the pressure for change. Under the pressure of acceleration, almost everything may become temporary, so that it can be continually adjusted to instrumental demands. Nothing is allowed to stand still, as the global economy is formed around a course of incessant competition. Temporary events also reflect the unregulated and unpredictable change, but they may also be hiccups in this process of expansion, filling the gaps left by structural adjustments, and forming the building blocks that pave the way for its growth. The future of the city becomes integrated with the future of the planet, as globalization proceeds and expands, turning all corners of the world into parts of a giant city, in which instrumental time is never allowed to slow down. Time is still flowing but at a pace that is faster than ever before, so as to make every moment a monetary asset.

Assigning numerical value helped reifying, institutionalizing and quantifying time. It was done through four historical processes of precision, systematization, materialization and collectivization of temporality. From relying on environmental observation to mechanical devices, from planetary movements to the subatomic world, technological innovation facilitated the ever-more precise ways of measuring time. Multiple local times were standardized into a single global framework, enabled by the emergence of the national and global powers. Time was objectified through finding material expression by the objects and devices that are used to keep time, from early sundials to digital and atomic clocks. Public displays of timekeeping devices, as well as the spatial organization of the social environment, have constituted a public infrastructure of time. Together, these four processes have led to the triumph of quantitative time in modern urban life, and the emergence of a universal time in which the entire world is envisaged as a sphere of simultaneity ruled by numbers. Temporary urbanism becomes the future of the city, where nothing can stand still, while always constrained within a grid of quantified, substantive time.

Long historical processes have been at work to construct a temporal infrastructure, present in all aspects of social life, from philosophy, religion and science to social institutions and conventions, and to the physical environment of cities and the natural world. This infrastructure has facilitated the regulation and management of change, integrating events into an overall framework of control and order. With the globalization of the last two centuries, this temporal framework has been expanded into most parts of the world. Time and space are reified, quantified and commodified so as to be available as instruments for economic productivity and political control. As these resources are finite, the key drive is to expand them, so as to enlarge the capacity for economic growth and political power. This spatiotemporal expansion finds its most dramatic manifestation in globalization.

Globalization is a spatial response to the limitations of time. When time and space are limited, they are expanded through various means: space is expanded through densification and relocation, while time is expanded through speed and multiplication. High-rise buildings and high-density cities, or relocating to the urban periphery, other parts of the same country of other parts of the world, where space is more abundant, are among the tools of overcoming spatial limitations. Instrumental time, meanwhile, is expanded through speed, where higher mobility and productivity are stimulated to do more in the time available, or multiplication of human time by employing larger numbers of people to undertake the same task. This expansion is made in the hope of reducing the mismatch between the activities at hand and the space-time available. Temporary urbanism is a contingent expansion of time and space, by providing the possibility of the multiple use of the same space, and of expanding time on a contingent basis. Experimentation, however, may be available to those who feel secure, rather than those who experience a contingent existence. The future of the city, in this context, would be increased contingency and precarity, particularly for the low-income and the low-skilled parts of the population, but increasingly also for those in the middle ground of the traditional social hierarchy.

Relational time

The second approach to time is relational, seeing it as the order of events. Thinkers from Aristotle to Leibniz and Einstein have doubted the existence of time as a metaphysical entity, arguing instead for thinking of time as a set of relationships between events. From this perspective, the event and its relationship with other events, and by extension the relationship between the observer and the world, occupy the centre stage. The order of events, and the way we experience and interpret them, rather than a metaphysical abstraction, becomes the basis of understanding time. The concept of time, like many other concepts, is an umbrella term for the totality of the various events, processes and experiences. Rather than a uniform and measurable entity, which is disrupted by unusual events, it is itself inductively built on the basis of a generalization of the experiences of these events. Like other concepts, therefore, it will be embedded in particular social and historical circumstances, rather than translating an ahistorical idea into practice.

The emphasis on events and their relationship offers the possibility of a transition from the mechanical to a social understanding of time. Time, like space, is a social phenomenon, subject to social processes that generate its concepts, regulates its application and consolidate its meanings. If time and space are envisaged as relationships, they become subject to the stabilizing effects of social institutions. Temporality is managed through the development of social institutions, the recurrent beliefs and modes of conduct that would generate continuity and predictability, helping to manage change and control events within a stable social framework. Some of these relational ideas overlap with and reflect the substantive notion of time.

When looked at from the perspective of social relations, temporary use of space, in this context, poses a challenge to the stability of the space-time arrangements, fixed forms of control and continuity of social institutions. Temporariness appears to have a disruptive impact on stable societies, somewhat similar to the impact of nomadic ways of life on sedentary populations. Temporariness remains a fundamental feature of all events, but here we can see how different orders of events may be identifiable, how they vary in their degree of rigidity and flexibility and how they are experienced by different observers. The future of the city may be envisaged as the emergence of alternative orders of events, rather than conforming to an image of permanence and perfection.

The imagined order of events has at times been expressed in geometrical shapes: cycles and lines. The cyclical order of events sees the past as being continually repeated and the future as a mere recurrence. The linear temporal order, in contrast, starts from a clear point of departure and moves forward towards progress or decline. Temporary events are either mere recurrences of previous events, or as signs of a change of direction. They may be seen as ruptures in the continuous line, an anomaly that may have the force to change the course of time; they may be seen as a new routine, breaking down the overall lines or cycles into many small pieces; or even an amorphous assemblage of events without any particular direction. In the relational framework, temporary events can be a change in the relationship, replacing one for another. Long-term relations are not avoided, and indeed short-term events may only pave the way for longer term arrangements. Short-term events may just be stepping stones to more stable circumstances.

In envisaging time as the relationship between events, the future of the city may be opened to alternative imaginations. The relationships can change, and it is possible to invent new relationships rather than following an eternal, inescapable path. While the relations may be subject to the strong and powerful forces that influence the course of events, a relational notion opens up the possibility of rethinking these arrangements and of the change of directions. The future is not necessarily a repetition of the past and is not destined to reach a preordained destination. It would be open for exploration and experimentation. Temporary urbanism, in this scenario, may be a vehicle of experimentation towards possible alternatives for the future of the city.

Intuitive time

A third perspective is the intuitive interpretation of time. While the substantive and relational concepts of time have been an integral part of the development of modern science, from Newton to Einstein, the third concept takes a categorical move away from positive science. The substantive and relational concepts of time tend to be third-person interpretations, while intuitive time is based on a first-person perspective. While the temporal fragments of events are linked together through an essence in substantive time and through a relation in relational time, they are connected through an experience in intuitive time.

The intuitive concept of time describes an embodied experience that finds meaning through the lived present, the relationship with the past and future, and the relationship with the material world. It is associated with a sense of anticipation as well as finitude, hope as well as anxiety, which is amplified through the acceleration of temporary events and the instability of the natural environment. Intuitive time is a sense of time as understood and experienced from a subjective perspective, in which consciousness unites the fragments of time, either as a narrative or as a primordial experience of unfolding temporality, bringing together the past, present and future into a holistic experience. It aims to go beyond the empiricist and positivist accounts and away from instrumental and quantitative concepts of time. Instead, it articulates a temporality which lies at the heart of existential meaning. The elemental sense of time forms an internal order of events, linking the sequential pieces together to construct temporal unity and continuity.

For the phenomenologists and existentialists, the subjective sense of time creates a coherent inner experience that could be described as the foundation of meaning. The fragments that constituted the empirical world could be woven together through consciousness and its unfolding temporality. The stability and coherence of this experience, however, is challenged on two fronts. The first challenge is by the acceleration of the world-time, which is expecting us to find meaning in ephemerality rather than continuity; and to cope with an ever-faster world of diversity and mobility. The psychological effects of the modern lifestyles on the human body and mind are well known, where the pressure for coping with speed and overcrowding is an everyday occurrence in large urban environments. In these circumstances, the embodied and embedded nature of intuitive time is challenged by the force of the mechanical grid of time and the ever-changing web of relational time. The human body and the body of the planet are both forced to adapt and be redefined as instruments to be used towards some functional goals. The environmental crisis and the global economy both create anxiety and instability for this embodied and embedded temporality.

The second challenge is from the relational time. The relational time, and more broadly the relational approach that redefines the concept of self and identity, shows that the self is not a coherent entity. The concept of a human mind, which is fully aware of itself and is in charge of the body and the world, has been undermined by the advances in neuroscience and psychology. The analysts of language have argued that the use of a public language to communicate undermines the authorship of the self, while psychoanalysts have emphasized the hidden world of the mind that shapes and influences ideas and behaviours without being visible. The human self is shaped by its relations with others and with the world, rather than evolving in isolation or emerging from a predetermined essence. The intuitive experience of time, therefore, becomes open and malleable, episodic and fragmented, rather than coherent and continuous.

Memories, as well as the material traces of the past, constitute a temporal storehouse which is integral to the city's time, always there to be explored, revived and reinterpreted. While modernity questioned this linkage to the past and tried to break it, the past survives in many forms of habits, social institutions and material environments. The link between temporal fragments, therefore, could be continually reconstructed through memory, unconscious and trace. In other words the intuitive sense of time uses the material environment to mediate between the multiple layers of time. In each situation, however, the past is reinvented, demonstrating an intention for continuity, rediscovering the possible vehicles that could facilitate such connections. The connections may also be attempts at inventing a new narrative identity, in the context of a global lexicon. Identity, however, is a relationship between similarity and difference, continuity and disruption; therefore irreducible to narrow narratives.

The mechanical, social and personal notions of time are all human time, but there is another time that is embedded in the material world, which may be called a no-time. Although the material non-human world is also subject to temporal ebbs and flows, from an intuitive perspective it is a manifestation of stability and continuity, rather than temporality and ephemerality. From the finite view of the intuitive perspective, things like mountains, seas and stones are all permanent and never-changing. Cities, and in particular the buildings in them, are an invented version of this embodied permanence, as the other side of the coin from the ephemeral events. Events are the soft and changing aspects of social life, which fill the void but are distinct from the mass, from the hard and sedimented materiality of architecture.

A paradoxical approach to the natural world has persisted throughout centuries: nature is thought to be simultaneously orderly and unruly, predictable and contingent, permanent and continually changing. The place of human beings in the natural world is also ambiguous: being part of it and yet assuming to be above it and aspiring to conquer it. Sometimes this paradox has been managed through a separation of the mind from the body, but it is a separation that cannot be held. The current environmental crisis has brought this paradox into sharper focus. When the reliable rock of the natural world is shaken and threatened, anxiety rises, rediscovering its contingent character and the vulnerability of the human species to its sudden changes. What seemed to be permanent becomes temporary, and the future of cities becomes laden with anxiety about inundation and pollution and, more generally, the conditions of life on earth. Anxiety, which has been described as a basic human condition towards the unknown future, is magnified when the stability of that future recedes at faster rates.

The different attitudes to nature can be seen in the struggle between classicism and romanticism. Classicism, which was revived in the Renaissance and the Enlightenment, looked to nature as the source of harmony and order, with hidden laws that could be discovered by science and controlled through technology. In contrast, romanticism, which partly drew on the medieval mindset, saw nature as the source of freedom from constraints, a place of diversity, originality and spontaneity. In this struggle, the notion of temporary urbanism would be interpreted as a moment of disorder by the classical tradition, while it might be seen as a source of emancipation by the romantic attitude. For the classical tradition, the future of the city would be orderly and harmonious, and a rupture in the course of events would jeopardize the future orderliness of the city. For the romantic tradition, in contrast, such a rupture would be an opening for new possibilities. It is partly along these romantic lines of taking refuge in the freedoms of the natural world that the escape from the city was initiated in the nineteenth century, as a precursor for the vast movement of suburbanization that is still unfolding.

At the detailed empirical level, all events may be interpreted as spatial-temporal fragments, each corresponding to a singular situation. When linked to one another, or when considered together as a whole, these events show change, from one situation to another. To make sense of this change, and to assign a name to events and their connections, the concept of time is created. This concept accounts for how situations are linked to one another, how change takes place and how this change follows a certain order, rather than being a collection of random accidents. All these concepts of time are ways of dealing with ephemerality. By building concepts, conventions, institutions and objects, the tide of ephemerality is pushed back and some ground is recovered to claim continuity and durability.

The mechanical theories of time see it as a sequence of quantified moments that constitute a flowing substance within an objective structure. In contrast, the personal and social senses of time offer alternative perspectives into the context and the conditions in which temporality is experienced. The first-person views of time develop alternative concepts of temporality which interpret it as phenomenological and existential, rather than abstract and instrumental. The social and interpersonal views, meanwhile, show how temporality is embedded in social practices, relations and conventions, as distinct from personal introspection or mechanical quantification. Temporary events may be seen as ruptures in these three overlapping and interpenetrating forms of temporality: mechanical, phenomenological and social. Temporary events become an integral part of the way time unfolds in the city: a disruption in the objective infrastructure of time, an inward exploration of temporal experience from the first-person perspective, and shifts and changes in the social sense of time in which the boundaries between what is permanent and what is temporary may be blurred.

All three concepts show attempts to produce durability out of ephemerality. An eternal substance, enduring social institutions and continuous personal experience are all linkages between singular events, in order to construct unity and permanence. At the same time, they are all open to the critique of multiplicity and break-up: the substance of time, the stability of the temporal grid, the solidity of the social conventions, and the internal coherence of the self and its memory and identity have all been opened to questioning. Time is always made of temporal multiplicities, and different forms of conceptual and practical linkages are made, supported by social narratives and public infrastructures of meaning, to weave these singularities together in a convincing way.

Temporariness, creativity and precarity

'Temporariness' is a broad term for a wide variety of meanings, some or all of which may be at work in any particular situation. In this section, first a summary of the processes of temporariness will be presented, followed by a particular focus on the interplay between the potentials for being creative and/or precarious.

Embedded, intentional and experiential temporariness

Temporary urbanism may be characterized by a high frequency of short-term events, in particular the temporary construction and use of space. While short-term events, and the temporary construction and use of space, have always existed, the increase in the rate of their occurrence and the spread of these occurrences across different parts of the world suggests that we have witnessed the emergence of a global trend. The processes of temporariness may have been embedded in human societies of all times, but its current increase of frequency is rooted in the particular conditions of our time. These conditions include intentional processes that aim at generating temporariness, and experiential conditions that are the consequences of these intentions.

Embedded temporariness refers to the basic ephemeral condition of all life. As such it includes all events that are an integral part of personal and social life, and can potentially be found in all places and times. They are the moments of everyday life in the city, which can take many different old and new forms. They are the result of accidental and unplanned encounters, or those that have long been established as social conventions. The examples include the temporary use of public space by groups of people to congregate and communicate, displays and parades by the organized institutions of power, and the construction of temporary structures for periodic events, festivals and street markets. These do not constitute a new trend and some of their forms can be as old as the city itself. The modern urban life, however, has increasingly intensified existential temporariness in a number of important ways.

Intentional temporariness refers to the changes that are the result of some planned actions. These planned actions may be instrumental or creative efforts that use temporariness as a tool or as an aim. The instrumental actions introduce practical adjustment to economic and social change. As new technologies are deployed and the nature of economic activity changes, older arrangements are treated as obsolete and exposed to a process of destruction and renewal. In this sense, all arrangements are treated as temporary, destined to be removed after the arrival of a more profitable and productive arrangement. Pragmatic use of space during the periods of economic contraction and oversupply of space gives rise to interim and provisional use of available spaces, filling the gaps left from economic shocks or periods of economic decline. In richer economies, these are expected to be short lived, but in the low-income economies this may lead to a more lasting form of existence. Creative actions, meanwhile, refer to those events that reflect a search for alternative arrangements, through critique and experimentation. The examples are the works of art that echo the existential conditions of ephemerality, raising questions about the status quo and experiment through displacement. The interim use of space for addressing the conditions of precarity, and searching for alternative ideas and practices by community groups are among the creative potentials of temporariness.

Experiential temporariness, in comparison, refers to those events that reflect the way temporariness is experienced in the urban space. It may be an experience of pleasure, facilitated by the changes in the quality of space and in the consumption of goods and services. The examples include the aesthetic animation of the urban environment through the use of colour and movement, as part of the attempts to improve the atmosphere of the city to make it a more pleasant place. This festivalization of the urban space is closely related to the rise of services as the most important activity of the urban economy in the global division of labour and the predominance of white-collar workers in this economy, with their own expectations about the urban life, and with consumerism as an engine of economic growth, fuelled by advertising. For the urban populations who are always on the move, nomadic urbanity brings about its own aesthetics, becoming a way of life. Rather than pleasure, precariousness and pain may be the condition of those who have a weak position in these circumstances and therefore are at the highest level of risk. Precarity is produced by the sheer pressure for higher productivity and faster paces of work within a global regime of temporal acceleration. Those parts of the population who suffer from precarity include low-income households, street traders, part-time workers, the homeless, the residents of informal settlements and those who have lost their homes to natural disasters, wars and persecution.

In any situation, there may be more than one of these three forms of temporariness at work, which shows the many-sided nature of temporary urbanism. While temporariness may become a fashionable trend, embraced by some as innovative and creative, it may impose the conditions of precarity on some others. The ambivalence of the trend, therefore, reveals the necessity of context-specific understanding and evaluation of any event.

Questioning, experimenting, innovating

While temporariness generates the conditions of precarity, it may also bring about the creative potential for transformation. I have explored these creative potentials under three groups: questioning, experimenting and innovating, each formed of a range of possibilities.

First, temporariness can question the status quo through displacement and break-up of structures. By displacing things from their familiar setting and conventional places, taken-for-granted ideas and practices are opened to critical inquiry and their legitimacy is tested. New possibilities may emerge through a change of perspective and an exploration of alternative arrangements. The place which is assigned to things is a framework that locates and traps them in particular circumstances, which may need to be challenged and transformed. Temporary events may be a sign of the structures crumbling into pieces, signalling the end of an era. The settled spatiotemporal structures and their institutional framework may be broken and their remnants may appear as floating fragments. Temporary events may also be the signs of the formation of a new reality, heralding a new set of arrangements that would replace the old ones. These new arrangements, however, are by no means guaranteed to be more advanced than the old ones, as they could lead to progressive as well as regressive outcomes.

The creative potential of ephemerality may also lie in its capacity for experimentation with ideas and practices, and its change of the way time and innovation are perceived. A change in perceiving time transforms Chronos to Kairos, quantitative to qualitative time, regulated occurrences to random, opportune moments. Time is understood as significant moments with disruptive and transformative effects. In a trend such as temporary urbanism, where such disruptive moments become the norm, the notion of innovation itself changes and fluidity rather than fixity becomes commonplace, simultaneously feeding consumerist innovation and precarious sociality. Disruptions may be part of a general process of random events, mistakes and accidents, which can only become significant if they show the possibility of easier interactions with the surrounding environment. They may also be the result of planned actions for change, which requires the mobilization of social forces towards desired directions.

The most significant spaces of temporary events in the city are public spaces, the crossroads which can facilitate social experimentation, affording contingency, expression and recognition. While they may be confined by physical and institutional frameworks, they are often kept empty of permanent features, where fixity and fluidity are combined so that public spaces can offer the possibility of alternative forms of expression and communication. The creative potential of the public space lies in its contingency, whereby the unplanned and the unexpected events can take place, and where diverse social forces may meet and new ideas and practices be developed. While these stages may help tame these social forces, it is also the place where these forces may take a central role and help change the city in fundamental ways.

Temporary events may contribute to the construction of meaning in ephemeral societies, in which the urban experience is no more than a travel through alienated landscapes. Through aesthetic experimentation, individual engagement with the environment, and the construction of social significance, short-term events can construct new meaning, even if it is itself ephemeral and short lived. Nevertheless, such meaning can go beyond the processes that produce this ephemerality, as the event is not limited to the conditions of its possibility, and can generate new meanings in unexpected ways.

Temporary urbanism may also be the sphere of innovating, testing new ideas and facilitating alternative practices conducted by civil society groups. Abandoned or contested places can offer the possibility of testing new ideas.

However, such experimentation may not be relied upon to become the primary form of service delivery and urban development, as they may not be automatically efficient and just. It would largely depend on who initiates, who manages, who benefits and under what conditions, that the creative potentials of temporary urbanism should be judged.

The most important form of evaluating temporary events is their impact on society and environment. Are these events initiated by some and have an adverse effect on others? The initiators may have any number of good reasons for their actions, but if the implications of these actions for others are somehow negative, then the action cannot be justified. It is not asking to try to please everyone, which will not be realistic, but minimizing the extent of negativity and harm to others. This may be a general point in evaluating any action, now extended to temporary events. If such events cause instability in the lives of people by forcing them to work harder, faster and under less favourable conditions; if it means initiating activities that gradually push some people out of their homes and neighbourhoods in a process of gentrification; and if it creates conditions of instability and precariousness in some individuals and groups, then it is an instrument of an overwhelmingly negative series of actions. On the other hand, if it opens up new spaces of questioning, experimenting and innovating towards reducing social and environmental vulnerability, these activities and events would find a completely different meaning.

References

Adam, Barbara, 1995, *Timewatch: The Social Analysis of Time*, Cambridge: Polity.

Aglietta, Michel, 2000, *A Theory of Capitalist Regulation: The US Experience*, New edition, London: Verso.

Alberti, Leon Battista, 1988, *On the Art of Building in Ten Books*, Cambridge, MA: The MIT Press.

Alexander, Christopher, Hajo Neis, Artemis Anninou, and Ingrid King, 1987, *A New Theory of Urban Design*, New York: Oxford University Press.

Alexander, Ella, 2012, Chanel comes to town, *Vogue*, 12 July 2012, http://www .vogue.co.uk/news/2012/07/12/chanel-opens-covent-garden-beauty-pop-up -store (accessed 17 November 2012).

Algra, Keimpe, 1995, *Concepts of Space in Greek Thought*, Leiden: E.J. Brill.

Anderson, Benedict, 1991, *Imagined Communities*, London: Verso.

Arendt, Hannah, 1958, *The Human Condition*, Chicago: University of Chicago Press.

Aristotle, 1996, *Physics*, Oxford: Oxford University Press.

Audi, Robert, ed., 1995, *The Cambridge Dictionary of Philosophy*, Cambridge: Cambridge University Press.

Aveni, Anthony, 2000, *Empires of Time: Calendars, Clocks and Cultures*, London: Tauris Parke Paperbacks.

Avery, Vivienne, Elaine Chamberlain, Carol Summerfield, and Linda Zealey, eds, 2007, *Focus on the Digital Age*, Office for National Statistics, London: Palgrave Macmillan.

Babere, Nelly, 2013, *Struggle for Space: Appropriation and Regulation of Prime Locations in Sustaining Informal Livelihoods in Dar Es Salaam City, Tanzania*, Unpublished PhD thesis, School of Architecture, Planning and Landscape, Newcastle upon Tyne: Newcastle University.

Bacon, Francis, 1995, 'The new science', in Isaac Kramnick, ed., *The Portable Enlightenment Reader*, New York: Penguin Books, pp. 39–42.

Badiou, Alain, 2005, *Being and Event*, London: Continuum.

Badiou, Alain, 2009, *Logic of Worlds: The Sequel to Being and Event*, London: Continuum.

Bakker, Martine, 2014, Sint-Antoniusvoorplein, *2014 Yearbook: Landscape Architecture and Urban Design in the Netherlands*, pp. 98–103, 155–156.

Banerjee, Robin and Patrick Jackson, 2012, China's ghost towns and phantom malls, *BBC*, http://www.bbc.co.uk/news/magazine-19049254 (accessed 24 May 2013).

Barber, Lionel, 2009, Capitalism redrawn, *Financial Times: The Future of Capitalism*, 12 May 2009, p. 3.

Bauman, Zygmunt, Adrian Franklin, and Ursula Biemann, 2010, *Transient Space: The Tourist Syndrome*, Berlin: Argo books.

BBC, 2012a, 'Empty shop rate rises across Britain as spending drops', *BBC News*, 4 September 2012, http://www.bbc.co.uk/news/business-19465725 (accessed 17 November 2012).

BBC, 2012b, 'Nottingham centre has "most vacant shop space"', *BBC News*, 4 September 2012, http://www.bbc.co.uk/news/uk-england -nottinghamshire-19470553 (accessed 17 November 2012).

BBC, 2012c, 'Dudley "worst among medium centres" for empty shops', *BBC News*, 4 September 2012, http://www.bbc.co.uk/news/uk-england -birmingham-19470562 (accessed 17 November 2012).

Bell, R.J. and D.T. Goldman, eds, 1986, *SI: The International System of Units*, National Physical Laboratory, London: HMSO.

Benjamin, Walter, 1999, *Illuminations*, London: Pimlico.

Bennett, Maxwell, Daniel Dennett, Peter Hacker, and John Searle, 2003, *Neuroscience and Philosophy: Brain, Mind and Language*, New York: Columbia University Press.

Berger, John, 1977, *Ways of Seeing*, London: British Broadcasting Corporation.

Bersgon, Henri, 2002, *Key Writings*, edited by Keith Ansell Pearson and John Mullarkey, London: Continnum.

Bishop, Peter and Lesley Williams, 2012, *The Temporary City*, London: Routledge.

Blackburn, Simon, 1996, *The Oxford Dictionary of Philosophy*, Oxford: Oxford University Press.

Bottéro, J., 2000, 'Religion and reasoning in Mesopotamia', in Jean Bottéro, Clarisse Herrenschmidt, and Jean-Pierre Vernant, eds, *Ancestor of the West: Writing, Reasoning and Religion in Mesopotamia, Elam and Greece*, Chicago: The University of Chicago Press, pp. 1–66.

Bouquet-Appel, Jean-Pierre, 2011, 'When the World's Population Took Off: The Springboard of the Neolithic Demographic Transition', *Science*, Vol. 333 (29 July), pp. 560–561.

Bourdieu, Pierre, 2000, *Pascalian Meditations*, Cambridge: Polity Press.

Boyer, Christine, 1996, *The City of Collective Memory*, Cambridge, MA: MIT Press.

Bradshaw, John, 1997, *Human Evolution: A Neuropsychological Perspective*, Hove: Psychology Press.

Briggs, Asa, 1968, *Victorian Cities*, Harmondsworth: Penguin.

Brignall, Miles, 2012, Spanish property: Polaris golf resort homes crash to a third of original price, *The Guardian*, 25 May 2012, http://www.guardian .co.uk/world/2012/may/25/spanish-property-polaris-homes-crash (accessed 1 September 2015).

British Retail Consortium, 2013, BRC/SPRINGBOARD Footfall and vacancies monitor April 2013: Shop vacancies reach a new high, http://www.brc.org.uk/ brc_news_detail.asp?id=2446&kCat=681&kData=2 (accessed 26 May 2013).

Brough, John, 1981, 'The phenomenology of internal time-consciousness', in Peter McCormick and Frederick Elliston, eds, *Husserl: Shorter Works*, Notre Dame, IN: University of Notre Dame Press, pp. 271–276.

Brown, Alison, 2006, *Contested Space: Street Trading, Public Space, and Livelihoods in Developing Cities*, Bourton on Dunsmore: Intermediate Technology Publications.

Brundtland, G.H., 1987, *Our Common Future*, Oxford: Oxford University Press.

Calladine, Dan, 2012, Advice and Resources, *London Pop-ups*, http://www .londonpopups.com/p/advice-resources.html (accessed 17 November 2012).

Čapek, M., ed., 1976, *The Concepts of Space and Time*, Dordrecht and Boston, MA: D.Reidel Publishing.

Castells, Manuel, 1996, *The Rise of the Network Society*, Oxford: Blackwell.

Cavanagh, Allison, 2007, *Sociology in the Age of the Internet*, Maidenhead: McGraw Hill/Open University Press.

Clare, John, 1984, *John Clare*, Oxford: Oxford University Press.

Colquhoun, Alan, 1989, *Modernity and the Classical Tradition: Architectural Essays 1980–1987*, Cambridge, MA: MIT Press.

Conzen, M.R.G., 1960, *Alnwick, Northumberland, a Study in Town-Plan Analysis*, London: IBG.

Cornford, F.M., 1976, 'The invention of space', in M. Čapek, ed., *The Concepts of Space and Time*, Boston Studies in the Philosophy of Science, Vol. XXII, Dordrecht and Boston, MA: D. Reidel Publishing, pp. 3–16.

Cottingham, J., 1992a, 'Cartesian dualism: Theology, metaphysics, and science', in J. Cottingham, ed., *The Cambridge Companion to Descartes*, Cambridge: Cambridge University Press, pp. 236–257.

Cottingham, J., 1992b, 'Introduction', in J. Cottingham, ed., *The Cambridge Companion to Descartes*, Cambridge: Cambridge University Press, pp. 1–20.

Coupe, Laurence, 2000, *The Green Studies Reader: From Romanticism to Ecocriticism*, London: Routledge.

Coveney, P. and R. Highfield, 1991, *The Arrow of Time: The Quest to Solve the Science's Greatest Mystery*, London: Flamingo.

Cox, George, 2005, *Cox Review of Creativity in Business: Building on the UK's Strengths*, London: HM Treasury/HMSO.

Curd, Patricia, 2012, 'Presocratic Philosophy', *The Stanford Encyclopedia of Philosophy* (Winter 2012 edition), Edward N. Zalta, ed., http://plato.stanford .edu/archives/win2012/entries/presocratics/ (accessed 1 September 2015).

Day, Paul, 2012, Crisis Draws Squatters to Spain's Empty Buildings, *Reuters*, 28 May 2012, http://uk.reuters.com/article/2012/05/28/uk-spain-squatters -idUKBRE84R09D20120528 (accessed 18 November 2012).

DCLG, 2009, *Looking after Our Town Centres*, London: Department for Communities and Local Government.

Debord, Guy, 1994, *The Society of the Spectacle*, New York: Zone Books.

Deleuze, Gilles, 1988, *Bergsonism*, New York: Zone Books.

Deleuze, Gilles and Felix Guattari, 1994, *What Is Philosophy?* New York: Columbia University Press.

Dennett, Daniel, 2013, *Intuition Pumps and Other Tools for Thinking*, London: Penguin books.

Descartes, René, 1968, *Discourse on Method and The Meditations*, London: Penguin.

Diani, Marco, ed., 1992, *The Immaterial Society: Design, Culture and Technology in the Postmodern World*, London: Prentice Hall.

Dries, Manuel, 2008, 'Towards Adualism: Becoming and nihilism in Nietzsche's philosophy', in Manuel Dries, ed., *Nietzsche on Time and History*, Berlin: Walter De Gruyter, pp. 113–145.

Durkheim, Emile, 1972a, *Emile Durkheim: Selected Writings*, edited by A. Giddens, Cambridge: Cambridge University Press.

Durkheim, Emile, 1972b, 'Forms of social solidarity', in Anthony Giddens, ed., *Emile Durkheim: Selected Writings*, Cambridge: Cambridge University Press, pp. 123–140.

Durkheim, Emile, 1972c, 'Methods of explanation and analysis', in Anthony Giddens, ed., *Emile Durkheim: Selected Writings*, Cambridge: Cambridge University Press, pp. 69–88.

Eberle, Martin, Robert Klanten, Hendrick Hellige, and M. Mischler, 2001, *Temporary Spaces*, Berlin: Die Gestalten Verlag.

EC, 2009a, *European Innovation Scoreboard 2008: Comparative Analysis of Innovation Performance*, Luxembourg: European Commission Enterprise and Industry, http://www.proinno-europe.eu/admin/uploaded_documents/EIS2008_Final_report-pv.pdf (accessed 17 October 2009).

EC, 2009b, *Europe's Information Society: Thematic Portal*, http://ec.europa.eu/information_society/services/ncg/en/index_en.htm (accessed 24 November 2009).

Einstein, Albert, 1954, 'Foreword', in M. Jammer, ed., *Concepts of Space: The History of Theories of Space in Physics*, Cambridge, MA: Harvard University Press, pp. xi–xvi.

Elton, L.R.B. and H. Messel, 1978, *Time and Man*, Oxford: Pergamon Press.

Empty Homes, 2013, Empty Homes Statistics 2011/12, http://www.emptyhomes.com/statistics-2/empty-homes-statistice-201112/ (accessed 24 May 2013).

Environment Agency, 2012, TE2100 Plan, London: Environment Agency.

Environment Agency, 2015, *The Thames Barrier*, https://www.gov.uk/the-thames-barrie (accessed 22 May 2015).

Epstein, Richard, 1998, *Principles for a Free Society: Reconciling Individual Liberty with the Common Good*, Reading, MA: Perseus Books.

Faber, Richard, 1983, *Foundations of Euclidean and Non-Euclidean Geometry*, New York: Marcel Dekker Inc.

Fidler, Eric, 2011, Temporary uses can enliven city neighborhoods, *Greater Greater Washington*, http://greatergreaterwashington.org/post/12674/temporary-uses-can-enliven-city-neighborhoods/ (accessed 26 May 2013).

Filarete, 1965, *Treatise on Architecture*, New Haven: Yale University Press.

Florida, Richard, 2002, *The Rise of the Creative Class*, New York: Basic Books.

Flynn, Finbarr, 2012, Ireland Bulldozes Ghost Estate in Life After Real Estate Bubble, *Bloomberg*, 20 July 2012, http://www.bloomberg.com/news/2012-07-19/ireland-bulldozes-ghost-estate-in-life-after-real-estate-bubble.html (accessed 18 November 2012).

Foucault, Michel, 1989, *The Archaeology of Knowledge*, Abingon: Routledge.

Foucault, Michel, 1993, 'Space, power and knowledge', in S. During, ed., *The Cultural Studies Reader*, London: Routledge, pp. 161–169.

Foucault, Michel, 2001, *Madness and Civilization*, London: Routledge.

Foucault, Michel, 2002, *The Order of Things*, London: Routledge.

Foucault, Michel, 2008, *The Birth of Biopolitics*, London: Palgrave Macmillan.

Freud, S., 1985, *Civilization, Society and Religion*, London: Penguin.

Fujita, M., P. Krugman, and A. Venebles, 1999, *The Spatial Economy: Cities, Regions and the International Trade*, Cambridge, MA: MIT Press.

Geppert, Alexander, 2013, *Fleeting Cities: Imperial Expositions in Fin-de-Siècle Europe*, London: Palgrave Macmillan.

Gershuny, J. and I. Miles, 1983, *The New Service Economy: The Transformation of Employment in Industrial Societies*, New York: Praeger Publishers.

Gethin, Rupert, 1998, *Foundations of Buddhism*, Oxford: Oxford University Press.

Giddens, A., 1984, *The Constitution of Society*, Cambridge: Polity Press.

Giedion, Sigfried, 1967, *Space, Time and Architecture: The Growth of a New Tradition*, Fifth edition, Cambridge, MA, Harvard University Press.

Gleick, J., 2000, *Faster: The Acceleration of Just about Everything*, London: Abacus.

Goffman, Erving, 1969, *The Presentation of Self in Everyday Life*, London: Allen Lane, The Penguin Press.

Goodall, Brian, 1987, *The Penguin Dictionary of Human Geography*, Harmondsworth: Penguin.

Govan, Fiona, 2012, The ghost towns of Spain: Images that are desolate symbols of collapsed property market, *The Telegraph*, 16 February 2012, http://www .telegraph.co.uk/news/worldnews/europe/spain/9087498/The-ghost-towns-of -Spain-Images-that-are-desolate-symbols-of-collapsed-property-market.html# (accessed 18 November 2012).

Gowans, Christopher, 2003, *Philosophy of the Buddha*, London: Routledge.

Graham, Steve, 1999, *Ice over the Poles*, Earth Observatory, http:// earthobservatory.nasa.gov/Features/PolarIce/polar_ice2.php (accessed 22 May 2015).

Gray, Jeremy, 1989, *Ideas of Space: Euclidean, Non-Euclidean and Relativistic*, Second edition, Oxford Science Publications, Oxford: Clarendon Press.

Greenfield, S., 2000, *The Private Life of the Brain*, London: Allen Lane, The Penguin Press.

Gregory, Derek, R.J. Johnston, Geraldine Pratt, Michael Watts, and Sarah Whatmore, 2009, *The Dictionary of Human Geography*, Fifth edition, Oxford: Wiley-Blackwell.

Habermas, Jürgen, 1984, *The Theory of Communicative Action*, London: Heinemann.

Habermas, Jürgen, 1989, *The Structural Transformation of the Public Sphere*, Cambridge, MA: MIT Press.

Halbwachs, Maurice, 1992, *On Collective Memory*, Chicago: Chicago University Press.

Hardt, Michael and Antonio Negri, 2000, *Empire*, Cambridge, MA: Harvard University Press.

Harvey, David, 1985, *The Urbanization of Capital*, Oxford: Blackwell.

Harvey, David, 1989, *The Condition of Postmodernity: An Enquiry into the Origins of Cultural Change*, Oxford: Blackwell.

Hawes, Louis, 1982, *Presences of Nature: British Landscape, 1780–1830*, New Haven, CT: Yale Center for British Art.

Hawking, Stephen, 1988, *A Brief History of Time: From the Big Bang to Black Holes*, London: Bantam.

Hawthorne, Christopher, 2012, From London Olympics to Pasadena, temporary architecture takes hold, *Los Angeles Times*, 28 July 2012.

Hegel, F., 1967, *Hegel's Philosophy of Right*, Oxford: Oxford University Press.

Heidegger, Martin, 1962, *Time and Being*, Oxford: Blackwell.

Heidegger, Martin, 1978, *Basic Writings*, edited by David Farrell Krell, London: Routledge.

Heidegger, Martin, 1996, *The Principle of Reason*, Bloomington: Indiana University Press.

Hellyer, Brian, 1974, *Man the Timekeeper*, East Sussex: Priory Press.

Hill, Jonathan, 2006, *Immaterial Architecture*, London: Routledge.

Hobbes, Thomas, 1985, *Leviathan*, London: Penguin.

Hobsbawm, E.J., 1990, *Nations and Nationalism Since 1780*, Second edition, Cambridge: Cambridge University Press.

Hollanders, Hugo and Adriana van Cruysen, 2009, *Design, Creativity and Innovation: A Scoreboard Approach*, February 2009, Pro Inno Europe Inno Metrics, http://www.proinno-europe.eu/admin/uploaded_documents/ EIS_2008_Creativity_and_Design.pdf (accessed 27 November 2009).

Hollis, Martin, 2002, *The Philosophy of Social Science*, Cambridge: Cambridge University Press.

Honneth, Axel, 1995, *The Struggle for Recognition: The Moral Grammar of Social Conflicts*, Cambridge: Polity Press.

Houlgate, Stephen, 1986, *Hegel, Nietzsche and the Criticism of Metaphysics*, Cambridge: Cambridge University Press.

Hume, David, 1985, *A Treatise of Human Nature*, London: Penguin.

Husserl, Edmund, 1981, 'The lectures on internal time-consciousness from the year 1905', in Peter McCormick and Frederick Elliston, eds, *Husserl: Shorter Works*, Notre Dame, IN: University of Notre Dame Press, pp. 277–288.

Husserl, Edmund, 1991, *On the Phenomenology of the Consciousness of Internal Time*, Dodrecht: Kluwer.

Ibne Mahmood, Shakeel Ahmed, 2012, 'Impact of Climate Change in Bangladesh: The Role of Public Administration and Government's Integrity', *Journal of Ecology and the Natural Environment*, Vol. 4, No. 8, pp. 223–240.

Institute for Urban Design, 2013, *Spontaneous Interventions*, http://www .spontaneousinterventions.org/ (accessed 20 May 2013).

IPCC, 2014, *Climate Change 2014: Synthesis Report. Contribution of Working Groups I, II and III to the Fifth Assessment Report of the Intergovernmental Panel on Climate Change* [Core Writing Team, R.K. Pachauri and L.A. Meyer, eds.], Geneva: IPCC.

ITU, 2009, *Measuring the Information Society: The ICT Development Index*, Geneva: International Telecommunication Union.

Jacobs, Jane, 1961, *The Death and Life of Great American Cities*, New York: Random House.

Jammer, Max, 1954, *Concepts of Space: The History of Theories of Space in Physics*, Cambridge, MA: Harvard University Press.

Janelle, D., 1968 'Central Place Development in a Time-Space Framework', *Professional Geographer*, 20, pp. 5–10.

Jenkins, Richard, 1996, *Social Identity*, London: Routledge.

Jodidio, Philip, 2011, *Temporary Architecture Now!* Taschen GmbH; Mul edition.

Johnston, R.J., D. Gregory, G. Pratt, and M. Watts, eds, 2000, *The Dictionary of Human Geography*, Fourth edition, Oxford: Blackwell.

Jordheim, Helge, 2007, 'Conceptual history between chronos and kairos – The case of "empire"', in K. Lindroos and Kari Palonen, eds, *Redescriptions. Yearbook of Political Thought and Conceptual History*, Vol. 11, Münster: LIT Verlag, pp. 115–145.

Jovis, 2007, *Urban Pioneers: Berlin Experience with Temporary Urbanism*, Jovis Verlag: Bilingual edition.

Kant, Immanuel, 1993, *Critique of Pure Reason*, London: JM Dent, Everyman.

Kant, Immanuel, 1995, 'What is enlightenment?' in Isaac Kraminck, ed., *Enlightenment Reader*, London: Penguin, pp. 1–7.

Kelly, Antoinette, 2011, Demolition the last resort for Ireland's 19,000 houses in ghost estates, *Irish Central*, 14 October 2011, http://www.irishcentral .com/news/Demolition-the-last-resort-for-Irelands-19000-houses-in-ghost -estates-131854748.html#axzz2CZlk0IzQ (accessed 18 November 2012).

Kierkegaard, Søren, 2014, *The Concept of Anxiety*, New York: Livernight.

Knox, P., 2005, 'Creating Ordinary Places: Slow Cities in a Fast World', *Journal of Urban Design*, Vol. 10, No. 1, pp. 1–11.

Kondratieff, N.D., 1935, 'The Long Waves in Economic Life', *The Review of Economic Statistics*, Vol. 17, No. 6, pp. 105–115.

Koolhaas, Rem, Bow-Wow, Rirkrit Tiravanija, Jung Yeondoo, and Hou Hanru, eds, 2008, *Transient City*, ActarD Inc.

Kuhn, Thomas, 1970, *The Structure of Scientific Revolutions*, Second edition, Chicago: The University of Chicago Press.

Lang Ho, Cathy, 2013, Intro, *Statements: Spontaneous Interventions*, http:// www.spontaneousinterventions.org/statements (accessed 26 May 2013).

Latour, Bruno, 1993, *We Have Never Been Modern*, New York: Harvester Wheatsheaf.

Lazzarato, M., 1996, 'Immaterial labour', in P. Virno and M. Hardt, eds, *Radial Thought in Italy*, Minneapolis: University of Minnesota Press.

Le Corbusier, 1986, *Towards a New Architecture*, New York: Dover Publications.

Le Corbusier, 1987, *The City of Tomorrow and Its Planning*, London: The Architectural Press.

Lefebvre, Henri, 1991, *The Production of Space*, Oxford: Blackwell.

Leibniz, Gottfried, 1979, 'The relational theory of space and time', in J.J.C. Smart, ed., *Problems of Space and Time*, New York: Macmillan, pp. 89–98.

Le Poidevin, Robin, 2007, *The Images of Time: An Essay on Temporal Representation*, Oxford: Oxford University Press.

Lindblom, Charles, 1959, 'The Science of "Muddling Through"', *Public Administration Review*, Vol. 19, No. 2, pp. 79–88.

Local Data Company, 2013, *The Knowledge Centre*, http://www .localdatacompany.com/knowledge (accessed 23 May 2013).

Locke, John, 1979, 'Place, extension and duration', in J.J.C. Smart, ed., *Problems of Space and Time*, New York: Macmillan, pp. 99–103.

London Pop-ups, 2012, *Jersey's Bohemia Pop-up at The Dorchester in Park Lane*, http://www.londonpopups.com/2012/03/jerseys-bohemia-pop-up-at-dorchester -in.html (accessed 22 January 2015).

Maclellan, Kylie and Andrew Osborn, 2015, Cameron woos voters with Thatcherite dream of home-owning democracy, *Reuters*, Tuesday, 14 April 2015, http://uk.reuters.com/article/2015/04/14/uk-britain-election -conservatives-idUKKBN0N42D120150414 (accessed 27 July 2015).

Madanipour, Ali, 1996, *Design of Urban Space*, Chichester: Wiley.

Madanipour, Ali, 2003, *Public and Private Spaces of Cities*, London: Routllege.

Madanipour, Ali, 2007, *Designing the City of Reason*, London: Routeldge.

Madanipour, Ali, 2009, 'City identity and management of change', in C. Vallat, F. Dufaux, and S. Kehman-Frisch, eds, *Pérennité urbaine, ou la ville par delà ses métamorphoses*, Paris: L'Harmattan, Vol. III, pp. 217–234.

Madanipour, Ali, ed., 2010, *Whose Public Space?* London: Routledge.

Madanipour, Ali, 2011, *Knowledge Economy and the City*, London: Routledge.

Madanipour, Ali, 2013, 'The identity of the city', in Silvia Serreli, ed., *City Project and Public Space*, Dodrecht: Springer, pp. 49–63.

Madanipour, Ali, 2014, *Urban Design, Space and Society*, London: Palgrave Macmillan.

Madanipour, Ali, 2016, 'Filarete', in Marco Sgarbi, ed., *Encyclopedia of Renaissance Philosophy*, New York: Springer.

Madanipour, Ali, G. Cars, and J. Allen, eds, 2003, *Social Exclusion in European Cities*, London: Routledge.

Madanipour, Ali, Sabine Knierbein, and Aglaee Degros, 2014, eds, *Public Space and the Challenges of Urban Transformation in Europe*, London: Routledge.

Maffesoli, M., 1996, *The Times of the Tribes*, London: Sage.

Markosian, Ned, 2014, 'Time', *The Stanford Encyclopedia of Philosophy* (Spring edition), Edward N. Zalta, ed. http://plato.stanford.edu/archives/spr2014/entries/time/ (accessed 1 September 2015).

Marx, Karl, 2008, *The Poverty of Philosophy*, New York: Cosimo Classics.

Marx, Karl and Friedrich Engels, 1930, *The Communist Manifesto of Karl Marx and Friedrich Engels*, edited by D. Ryazanoff, London: Martin Lawrence Ltd.

Marx, Karl and Frederick Engels, 1968, *Selected Works*, London: Lawrence and Wishart.

Massey, Doreen, 2005, *For Space*, London: Sage.

McDonough, Tom, 2002, *Guy Debord and the Situationist International: Texts and Documents*, Cambridge, MA: MIT Press.

McKusick, James, 2000, *Green Writing: Romanticism and Ecology*, London: Macmillan.

McLuhan, Marshall, 1964, *Understanding Media: The Extensions of Man*, London: Routledge & Kegan Paul.

Mill, John Stuart, 1974, *On Liberty*, London: Penguin Books.

Nayar, Pramod, 2010, *The New Media and Cybercultures Anthology*, Oxford: Blackwell.

NEF, 2010, *Re-imagining the High Street: Escape from Clone Town Britain*, London: New Economics Foundation.

Nerlich, Graham, 1994, *The Shape of Space*, Second edition, Cambridge: Cambridge University Press.

Newton, Isaac, 1995, 'Mathematical principles of natural philosophy', in Isaac Kraminck, ed., *Enlightenment Reader*, London: Penguin, pp. 43–47.

Nicholas, David, 2000, *Assessing Information Needs: Tools, Techniques and Concepts for the Internet Age*, London: Aslib Information Management.

Nietzsche, Friedrich, 1989, *On the Genealogy of Morals: Ecce Homo*, New York: Vintage.

Norberg-Schultz, Christian, 1980, *Meaning in Western Architecture*, London: Studio Vista.

Nylander, Johan, 2013, World's biggest mall a China 'ghost town', *CNN*, http://edition.cnn.com/2013/03/03/business/china-worlds-largest-mall (accessed 24 May 2013).

O'Sullivan, Arthur, 2012, *Urban Economics*, Eighth edition, New York: McGraw-Hill Higher Education.

OECD, 1996, *The Knowledge-Based Economy*, Paris: Organization for Economic Cooperation and Development.

Ofcom, 2013, *UK consumers are a nation of online shoppers*, http://consumers.ofcom.org.uk/2011/12/uk-consumers-are-a-nation-of-online-shoppers/ (accessed 24 May 2013).

Olson, Eric T., 2002, 'Personal Identity', *The Stanford Encyclopedia of Philosophy* (Fall 2002 edition), Edward N. Zalta, ed. http://plato.stanford.edu/archives/fall2002/entries/identity-personal/ (accessed 1 September 2015).

Osborne, Hilary, 2015, 'Generation rent: The housing ladder starts to collapse for the under-40s', *The Guardian*, http://www.theguardian.com/money/2015/jul/22/pwc-report-generation-rent-to-grow-over-next-decade (accessed 27 July 2015).

Oswalt, Philipp, Klaus Overmeyer, and Philipp Misselwitz, 2013, *Urban Catalyst: The Power of Temporary Use*, Berlin: JOVIS Verlag (accessed 1 March 2013).

Paris Municipality, *Paris Plages*, http://www.paris.fr/english/visit/highlights/paris-plages/rub_8208_stand_34146_port_18969 (accessed 20 May 2013).

Parsons, Talcott, 1952, *The Social System*, London: Tavistock Publications.

Patton, Paul, 2010, *Deleuzian Concepts*, Stanford, CA: Stanford University Press.

Perez, Carlota, 1983, Structural change and assimilation of new technologies in the economic and social systems, *Futures*, October 1983, pp. 357–375.

Pevsner, Nikolaus, 1963, *An Outline of European Architecture*, Seventh edition, Harmondsworth: Penguin Books.

Pivcevic, Edo, 1970, *Husserl and Phenomenology*, London: Hutchinson.

Plato, 1977, *Timaeus and Critias*, London: Penguin Books.

Plato, 1982, *The Collected Dialogues of Plato*, edited by Edith Hamilton and Huntington Cairns, Princeton, NJ: Princeton University Press.

Plato, 1993, *Republic*, Oxford: Oxford University Press.

Portas, Mary, 2011, *The Portas Review: An Independent Review into the Future of our High Streets*, London: Department for Business, Innovation and Skills.

Punter, J., ed., 2010, *Urban Design and the British Urban Renaissance*, London: Routledge.

Quah, Danny, 2002, 'Matching Demand and Supply in a Weightless Economy: Market-Driven Creativity with and without IPRS', *De Economist*, Vol. 150, No. 4, pp. 381–403.

Quinton, A., 2005, 'Romanticism, philosophical', in T. Honderich, ed., *The Oxford Companion to Philosophy*, Oxford: Oxford University Press.

Rahula, Walpola, 1974, *What the Buddha Taught*, New York: Green Press.

Raymer, Michael, 2009, *The Silicon Web: Physics for the Internet Age*, London: Taylor & Francis.

Rees, William, 2014, 'Avoiding collapse: An agenda for de-growth and re-localisation', in S. Davoudi and A. Madanipour, eds, *Reconsidering Localism*, London: Routledge, pp. 193–215.

Regent Street Partnership, 2013, *2012 on Regent Street*, http://www.regentstreetonline.com/Feature-Articles/2012-on-Regent-Street.aspx (accessed 20 May 2013).

Rice, Doyle and Alia Dastagir, 2013, One year after Sandy, 9 devastating facts, *USA Today*, 29 October 2013.

Ricoeur, Paul, 1995, *Oneself as Another*, Chicago: Chicago University Press.

Ricoeur, Paul, 2007, *The Course of Recognition*, Cambridge, MA: Harvard University Press.

Rossi, Aldo, 1982, *The Architecture of the City*, Cambridge, MA: MIT Press.

Rousseau, Jean-Jacques, 1968, *The Social Contract*, London: Penguin.

Ruddick, Graham, 2008, Empty office space in City of London rises by almost 50pc, *The Telegraph*, http://www.telegraph.co.uk/finance/3117037/Empty-office-space-in-City-of-London-rises-by-almost-50pc.html (accessed 26 May 2013).

Ruddick, Graham, 2009, London's empty office space tops 10m sq ft, *The Telegraph*, http://www.telegraph.co.uk/finance/recession/5126359/Londons-empty-office-space-tops-10m-sq-ft.html (accessed 26 May 2013).

Saalman, Howard, 1968, *Medieval Cities*, London: Studio Vista.

Sartre, Jean Paul, 2003, *Being and Nothingness*, London: Routledge.

Scardino, Barrie, William F. Stern, and Bruce Webb, eds, 2004, *Ephemeral City: 'Cite' Looks at Houston*, Austin: University of Texas Press.

Schacht, R., 1996 'Nietzsche's kind of philosophy', in Bernard Magnus and Kathleen Higgins, eds, *The Cambridge Companion to Nietzsche*, Cambridge: Cambridge University Press.

Schumpeter, Joseph, 2003, *Capitalism, Socialism and Democracy*, London: Taylor and Francis.

Schutz, Alfred, 1970, *On Phenomenology and Social Relations: Selected Writings*, Chicago: Chicago University Press.

Searle, John, 1995, *The Construction of Social Reality*, London: Penguin.

Searle, John, 1999, *Mind, Language and Society: Philosophy in the Real World*, London: Weidenfeld and Nicolson.

Sert, Jose Luis, 1944, *Can Our Cities Survive? An ABC of Urban Problems, Their Analysis, Their Solution*, Cambridge, MA: Harvard University Press.

Skinner, Quentin, 1981, *Machiavelli: A Very Short Introduction*, Oxford: Oxford University Press.

Slow Food, 2006, 'Introduction', *Slow Food*, www.slowfood.com (accessed 1 March 2006).

Slowik, Edward, 2014, 'Descartes' Physics', *The Stanford Encyclopedia of Philosophy* (Summer 2014 edition), Edward N. Zalta, ed., http://plato.stanford .edu/archives/sum2014/entries/descartes-physics/ (accessed 1 September 2015).

Smart, J.J.C., ed., 1979, *Problems of Space and Time*, New York: Macmillan.

Smith, Adam, 1993, *An Inquiry into the Nature and Cause of the Wealth of Nations*, ed. Kathryn Sutherland, Oxford: Oxford University Press.

Smith, Daniel and Henry Somers-Hall, 2012, *The Cambridge Companion to Deleuze*, Cambridge: Cambridge University Press.

Smith, John E., 1986, 'Time and Qualitative Time', *The Review of Metaphysics*, Vol. 40, No. 1 (September), pp. 3–16.

Spencer, Richard, 2010, Dubai may have to knock down buildings constructed during boom, *The Telegraph*, http://www.telegraph.co.uk/news/worldnews/ middleeast/dubai/8013438/Dubai-may-have-to-knock-down-buildings -constructed-during-boom.html (accessed 24 May 2013).

Stiglitz, Joseph, 1999, *Public Policy for a Knowledge Economy*, Washington, DC: World Bank, http://www.worldbank.org/html/extdr/extme/jssp012799a.htm (accessed 6 July 2009).

Taylor, Charles, 1979, *Hegel and Modern Society*, Cambridge: Cambridge University Press.

Taylor, Charles, 1989, *Sources of the Self: The Making of the Modern Identity*, Cambridge: Cambridge University Press.

Taylor, Charles, 1994, 'The politics of recognition', in C. Taylor and A. Gutman, eds, *Multiculturalism: Examining the Politics of Recognition*, Princeton: Princeton University Press, pp. 25–73.

Temel, Robert and Florian Haydn, eds, 2006, *Temporary Urban Spaces: Concepts for the Use of City Spaces*, Basel: Birkhauser Verlag AG.

Thacker, Christopher, 1983, *The Wildness Pleases: The Origins of Romanticism*, London: Croom Helm.

Thomas, Maureen, 2008, 'Digitality and Immaterial Culture: What Did Viking Women Think?' *International Journal of Digital Culture and Electronic Tourism*, Vol. 1, No. 2/3, pp. 177–191.

Time Service Department, 2014, *Weighted Clocks Currently in the USNO Time Scale*, US Naval Observatory, http://tycho.usno.navy.mil/cgi-bin/clock-count.pl (accessed 12 December 2014).

Torretti, Roberto, 1984, *The Philosophy of Geometry from Reimann to Poincaré*, Dodrecht: D.Reidel Publishing.

Tschumi, Bernard, 2010, *Event-Cities 4*, Cambridge, MA: MIT Press.

Turetzky, Philip, 1998, *Time*, London: Routledge.

Turner, Bryan S., 2006, *The Cambridge Dictionary of Sociology*, Cambridge: Cambridge University Press.

Tuvalu, 2010, *Tuvalu and Global Warming*, http://www.tuvaluislands.com/warming .htm (accesed 22 May 2015).

UNESCO, 2005, *Towards Knowledge Societies*, UNESCO World Report, Paris: United Nations Educational, Scientific and Cultural Organization (UNESCO).

Urban Task Force, 1999, *Towards Urban Renaissance*, London: E&F Spon.

Virilio, Paul, 1986, *Speed and Politics*, New York: Semiotext(e).

Vitruvius, 1999, *Ten Books on Architecture*, Cambridge: Cambridge University Press.

Weber, Max, 1978, *Economy and Society: An Outline of Interpretive Sociology*, Berkeley: University of California Press.

Weitzel, Antje, 2011, *Transient Spaces*, Berlin: Argo Books.

Wells, Alan, 1970, *Social Institutions*, London: Heinemann.

Whitehand, J.W.R., 1987, 'Recent developments in urban morphology', in Dietrich Denecke and Gareth Shaw, eds, *Urban Historical Geography: Recent Progress in Britain and Germany*, Cambridge: Cambridge University Press, pp. 285–296.

Whitrow, G.J., 1972, *What Is Time?* London: Thames and Hudson.

Williams, R., 1985, *Keywords: A Vocabulary of Culture and Society*, Oxford: Oxford University Press.

Wittkower, Rudolf, 1938, 'Chance, Time and Virtue', *Journal of the Warburg Institute*, Vol. 1, No. 4 (April), pp. 313–321.

WJS, 2011, Detroit's Population Crashes, *The Wall Street Journal*, http://online .wsj.com/article/SB10001424052748704461304576216850733151470.html#p roject%3Ddetroit0311%26articleTabs%3Dinteractive (accessed 24 May 2013).

Zammito, John, 2004, 'Koselleck's Philosophy of Historical Time(s) and the Practice of History Zeitschichten: Studien zur Historik (Mit einem Beitrag von Hans-Georg Gadamer) by Reinhart Koselleck, Book Review', *History and Theory*, Vol. 43, No. 1 (February), pp. 124–135.

Zander, Thomas, ed., 2008, *Jean Paul Deridder: Stadt Der Kinder, Berlin, City of Transience*, Hatje Cantz; Bilingual edition.

Ziehl, Michael, Sarah Osswald, Oliver Hasemann, and Daniel Schnier, eds, 2012, *Second Hand Spaces: Recycling Sites Undergoing Urban Transformation*, Berlin: JOVIS Verlag.

Žižek, Slavoj., 1999, *The Ticklish Subject: The Absent Centre of Political Ontology*, London: Verso.

Žižek, Slavoj, 2014, *Event: Philosophy in Transit*, London: Penguin.

Index